Gann Trade Real Time

By Larry Jacobs

Published by Hallikers' Inc

TABLE OF CONTENTS

Gann Trade Real Time 1
GETTING STARTED 7
W. D. GANN TICKER MAGAZINE ARTICLE 9
W.D. GANN A LEGEND by Les Clemens 18
COMPUTER 31
COMPUTER CHAIR 32
PSYCHOLOGY OF TRADING 33
THE RIGHT KIND OF CHARTS 36
TRADING SOFTWARE 43
INTRADAY TREND – PRICE ACTION 45
INTRADAY TRENDS – TIME ACTION 48
UNIT MOVES 50
POINTS MOVE 52
MATHEMATICS 54
THE CUBE 57
RETRACEMENTS – 30-MIN CHART 59
THREE BASIC SHAPES 61
90 SQUARE CHART 63
CONSTRUCTING CHARTS PROPERLY 65
THE 1X1 ANGLE 67
GANN ANGLES 74
THE TIME FACTOR 83
BUILT UP FORCES 86
HARMONICS 87
TXN DAILY CHART OVERLAY 91
FINDING THE MAIN TREND 92

MONTHLY MOVES	94
MARKET ACTION	95
LONG-TERM SUPPORT AND RESISTANCE	98
TIME AND PRICE OVERLAYS	102
CHARTS	115
HOW TO USE THE OVERLAY GANN SQUARE	117
TIME AND PRICE CHARTS	119
Here is How to Use the Overlay	124
TABLE CHARTS	125
FORECASTING TIME	134
HARMOMICS OF THESE CYCLES	137
SHIFTS IN CYCLES	139
REOCURRING CYCLES	141
ELLIOTT WAVE THEORY	142
USING GANN RATIOS	145
FORECASTING PRICE	146
USING CIRCLE NUMBERS FROM BEGINNING NUMBERS	150
MMM DAILY CHART T&P SQUARING	152
MMM DAILY CHART SEASONALS	154
SQUARE OF NINE FIXED AND SEASONALS	155
TXN 5-MIN CHART AND THE FIXED SQUARE OF NINE	156
TXN 5-MIN CHART AND THE FIXED SQ OF NINE WITH CHANNELS	157
TXN 5-MIN FIXED SQ OF NINE WITH CHANNELS AND VARIABLE	158
PYRAPOINT TOOL	160
GANN'S SECRET PYTHAGOREAN SQUARE	161
GANN'S ROAD MAP APPROACH	173
PYRAPOINT TIME AND PRICE	178

CHART PATTERNS..188
TXN 5-MIN CHART RIGHT ANGLE BROADENING FORMATION...189
SBC 5-MIN RIGHT ANGLE DESCENDING BROADENING FORMATION...190
SBC 5-MIN BROADING TOP..191
SBC 5-MIN CHART ASCENDING BROADENING WEDGE 192
ORCL 5-MIN CHART DESCENDING BROADENING WEDGE 193
MMM 5-MIN CUP HANDLE FORMATION............................194
MRK 30-MIN CHART DEAD BOUNCE..................................195
MRK 30-MIN DIAMOND TOP..196
MMM 30-MIN DIAMOND CONTINUATION.........................197
MCD 30-MIN CHART DIAMOND BOTTOM.........................198
SP Z1 15-MIN CHART DOUBLE BOTTOM............................199
SP Z1 15-MIN CHART DOUBLE TOP....................................200
EZ 15-MIN CHART BREAKAWAY GAP................................201
DISNEY 15-MIN CHART MIDWAY GAP...............................202
EXHAUSTION GAP..203
ES Z1 5-MIN CHART HEAD AND SHOULDERS TOP..........204
ES Z1 15-MIN CHART HEAD AND SHOULDERS BOTTOM 205
KO 60-MIN CHART INSIDE/OUTSIDE DAYS......................206
MSFT DAILY CHART ISLAND REVERSAL.........................207
PG 30-MIN CHART RECTANGLE BOTTOM........................208
IP 30-MIN CHART RECTANGLE TOP..................................209
DIS 5-MIN CHART RECTANGLE MIDDLE..........................210
DIS 15-MIN CHART ROUNDING BOTTOM.........................211
HD 5-MIN CHART DOWN TREND SCALLOP.....................213
HD 5-MIN SCALLOP UPTREND...214

Entry	Page
INTC 5-MIN CHART ASCENDING TRIANGLE	215
GE 5-MIN CHART DESCENDING TRIANGLE	216
DD 5-MIN CHART SYMMETRICAL TOP	217
EK 30-MIN CHART SYMMETRICAL BOTTOM	218
T 15-MIN CHART TRIPLE TOP	219
ORCL 30-MIN CHART TRIPLE BOTTOM	220
MRK 30-MIN CHART FALLING WEDGE	221
MRK 30-MIN CHART RISING WEDGE	222
PRICE – RETRACEMENTS	223
PRICE – RETRACEMENTS – TWO AT THE SAME TIME	225
MSFT 30 MINUTE CHART	226
79 PERCENT RETRACEMENT	227
MMM 30 MINUTE 50% RETRACEMENT	228
MMM 30 MINUTE CHART 200% RETRACEMENT	229
PRICE PROJECTION 1	230
PRICE PROJECTION 2	231
PRICE PROJECTION 3	232
ORCL 30-MIN CHART 3 RETRACEMENTS	233
MCD 30-MIN % RETRACEMENT 1	234
MCD 30-MIN % RETRACEMENT 2	235
MRK 30-MIN TIME RETRACEMENT	236
PG 30-MIN CHART TIME ANALYSIS	237
PFE 5-MIN CHART FIBONACCI CYCLES 34 AND 55	238
ORCL 30-MIN CHART GANN CYCLE NUMBERS	239
SBC 30-MIN 40 CYCLE PERIOD	240
SBC 30-MIN CHART 40 CYCLE PERIOD X 3	241
MSFT 60-MIN CHART WITH 5 ELLIOTT WAVES	242
ES Z1 6—MIN CHART WITH ABC ELLIOTT WAVES	243
SWING CHARTS	244

DOUBLE AND TRIPLE TOPS AND BOTTOMS 247
VOLUME AND OPEN INTEREST 249
GANN CHANNELS 252
CAPITAL REQUIRED 254
TYPES OF ORDERS 257
MAKING IT WORK 260
Copyright 262

GETTING STARTED

In the past three years you have heard about the new day-traders. Many new people quitting their professions to start a new career in day trading. They buy expensive computers, hook up to high-speed Internet access and start trading with limited capital. Even housewives were using their grocery money during the weeks in hopes of making money. Some retired people put their entire life saving on the line day trading and lost it all. The reason most of these people have lost or will lose is their trading is not based on sound mathematical principals, but rather just seat-of-their-pants gambling. The methods they trade on are not scientific nor are the methods back tested for any degree of time.

When you opened this book you took the one step that will help you learn how to be successful at the most desirable, but hardest professionals in the world. That profession is real time trading. This book is not going to give you an instant secret to day trading. It is going to give you the basics so that you might start the path to understanding how the markets work both short term and long term. You need to know and fully understand the markets and develop successful trading strategies to become successful at this endeavor. Knowledge of the markets must be combined with discipline to effectively control you emotions to stick to what you have learned and consistently make money in the markets. Most people have lost money in the markets due to several simple mistakes. You can prevail over that market and overcome these mistakes. This book will also teach you how to understand, distinguish and stay steer clear of these common mistakes.

If you are just getting started or if you are an experience trader, you will find this book a very practical guide. You'll learn the basics from hardware and software to getting the right brokerage firm. You learn how to use the right kind of orders for your trades.

It is our sincere wish that you learn how to successful trade the markets in the real-time trading atmosphere. By the end of the book, we hope that we have made it easier, less risky and a more lucrative endeavor.

To keep on to learn about trading we would like you to visit our website www.tradersworld.com. This is the official website of Traders World magazine which has been published since 1981. There you will find many articles and information about methods of trading from hundreds of writers.

To understand how successful W.D. Gann was please read the following two articles: W.D. Gann Ticker Magazine Article and W.D. Gann a Legend.

W. D. GANN TICKER MAGAZINE ARTICLE

Reprinted from an Article of The Ticker and Investment Digest Featuring W.D. Gann dated December 1909

Sometime ago the attention of this magazine was attracted by certain long pull Stock Market predictions, which were being made by William D. Gann. In a large number of cases Mr. Gann gave us, in advance, the exact points at which certain stocks and commodities would sell, together with prices close to the then prevailing figures which would not be touched.

For instance, when the New York Central was 131 he predicted that it would sell at 145 before 129. So repeatedly did his figures prove to be accurate, and so different did his work appear from that of any expert whose methods we had examined, that we set about to investigate Mr. Gann and his way of figuring out these predictions, as well as the particular use which he was making of them in the market.

The results of this investigation are remarkable in many ways.

It appears to be a fact Mr. W. D. Gann has developed an entirely new idea as to the principles governing stock market movements. He bases his operations upon certain natural laws, which, though existing since the world began, have only in recent years been subjected to the will of man and added to the list of so-called modern discoveries. We have asked Mr. Gann for an outline of his work, and have secured some remarkable evidence as to the results obtained there from.

We submit this in full recognition of the fact that in Wall Street a man with a new idea, an idea which violates the traditions and encourages a scientific view of the Proposition, is not usually welcomed by the majority, for the reason that he stimulates thought and research. These activities the said majority abhors.

W. D. Gann's description of his experience and methods is given herewith. It should be read with recognition of the established fact that Mr. Gann's predictions have proved correct in a large majority of instances.

"For the past ten years I have devoted my entire time and attention to the speculative markets. Like many others, I lost thousands of dollars and experienced the usual ups and downs incidental to the novice who enters the market without preparatory knowledge of the subject."

"I soon began to realize that all successful men, whether Lawyers, Doctors or Scientists, devoted years of time to the study and investigation of their particular pursuit or profession before attempting to make any money out of it."

"Being in the Brokerage business myself and handling large accounts, I had opportunities seldom afforded the ordinary man for studying the cause of success and failure in the speculations of others. I found that over ninety percent of the traders who go into the market without knowledge or study usually lose in the end."

"I soon began to note the periodical recurrence of the rise and fall in stocks and commodities. This led me to conclude that natural law was the basis of market movements. I then decided to devote ten years of my life to the study of natural law as applicable to the speculative markets and to devote my best energies toward making speculation a profitable profession. After exhaustive researches and investigations of the known sciences, I discovered that the law of vibration enabled me to accurately determine the exact points at which stocks or commodities should rise and fall within a given time."

The working out of this law determines the cause and predicts the effect long before the street is aware of either. Most speculators can testify to the fact that it is looking at the effect and ignoring the cause that has produced their losses.

"It is impossible here to give an adequate idea of the law of vibrations as I apply it to the markets. However, the layman may be able to grasp some of the principles when I state that the law of vibration is the fundamental law upon which wireless telegraphy, wireless telephone and phonographs are based. Without the existence of this law the above inventions would have been impossible."

"In order to test the efficiency of my idea I have not only put in years of labor in the regular way, but I spent nine months working night and day in the Astor Library in New York and in the British Museum of London, going over the records of stock transactions as far back as 1820. I have incidentally examined the manipulations of Jay Gould, Daniel Drew, Commodore Vanderbilt & all other important manipulators from that time to the present day. I have examined every quotation of Union Pacific prior to & from the time of E. H. Harriman, Mr. Harriman's was the most masterly. The figures show that, whether unconsciously or not, Mr. Harriman worked strictly in accordance with natural law."

"In going over the history of markets and the great mass of related statistics, it soon becomes apparent that certain laws govern the changes and variations in the value of stocks, and that there exists a periodic or cyclic law which is at the back of all these movements. Observation has shown that there are regular periods of intense activity on the Exchange followed by periods of inactivity."

Mr. Henry Hall in his recent book devoted much space to "Cycles of Prosperity and Depression," which he found recurring at regular intervals of time. The law, which I have applied, will not only give these long cycles or swings, but the daily and even hourly movements of stocks. By knowing the exact vibration of each individual stock I am able to determine at what point each will receive support and at what point the greatest resistance is to be met.

"Those in close touch with the market have noticed the phenomena of ebb and flow, or rise and fall, in the value of stocks. At certain times a stock will become intensely active, large transactions being made in it; at other times this same stock will become practically stationary or inactive with a very small volume of sales. I have found that the law of vibration governs and controls these conditions. I have also found that certain phases of this law govern the rise in a stock and an entirely different rule operates on the decline."

"While Union Pacific and other railroad stocks which made their high prices in August were declining, United States Steel Common was steadily advancing. The law of vibration was at work, sending a particular stock on the upward trend whilst others were trending downward."

"I have found that in the stock itself exists its harmonic or inharmonious relationship to the driving power or force behind it. The secret of all its activity is therefore apparent. By my method I can determine the vibration of each stock and also, by taking certain time values into consideration, I can, in the majority of cases, tell exactly what the stock will do under given conditions."

"The power to determine the trend of the market is due to my knowledge of the characteristics of each individual stock and a certain grouping of different stocks under their proper rates of vibration. Stocks are like electrons, atoms and molecules, which hold persistently to their own individuality in response to the fundamental law of vibration. Science teaches that 'an original impulse of any kind finally resolves itself into a periodic or rhythmical motion; also, just as the pendulum returns again in its swing, just as the moon returns in its orbit, just as the advancing year over brings the rose of spring, so do the properties of the elements periodically recur as the weight of the atoms rises."

"From my extensive investigations, studies and applied tests, I find that not only do the various stocks vibrate, but that the driving forces controlling the stocks are also in a state of vibration. These vibratory forces can only be known by the movements they generate on the stocks and their values in the market. Since all great swings or movements of the market are cyclic, they act in accordance with periodic law."

"Science has laid down the principle that the properties of an element are a periodic function of its atomic weight. A famous scientist has stated that 'we are brought to the conviction that diversity in phenomenal nature in its different kingdoms is most intimately associated with numerical relationship. The numbers are not intermixed accidentally but are subject to regular periodicity. The changes and developments are seen to be in many cases as somewhat odd."

Thus, I affirm every class of phenomena, whether in nature or on the stock market, must be subject to the universal law of causation and harmony. Every effect must have an adequate cause.

"If we wish to avert failure in speculation we must deal with causes. Everything in existence is based on exact proportion and perfect relationship. There is no chance in nature, because mathematical principles of the highest order lie at the foundation of all things. Faraday said, "There is nothing in the universe but mathematical points of force."

"Vibration is fundamental: nothing is exempt from this law. It is universal, therefore applicable to every class of phenomena on the globe."

Through the law of vibration every stock in the market moves in its own distinctive sphere of activities, as to intensity, volume and direction; all the essential qualities of its evolution are characterized in its own rate of vibration. Stocks, like atoms, are really centers of energy; therefore, they are controlled mathematically. Stocks create their own field of action and power: power to attract and repel, which principle explains why certain stocks at times lead the market and 'turn dead' at other times. Thus, to speculate scientifically it is absolutely necessary to follow natural law.

"After years of patient study I have proven to my entire satisfaction, as well as demonstrated to others, that vibration explains every possible phase and condition of the market."

In order to substantiate Mr. W. D. Gann's claims as to what he has been able to do under his method, we called upon Mr. William E. Gilley, an Inspector of Imports, 16 Beaver Street, New York. Mr. Gilley is well known in the downtown district. He himself has studied stock market movements for twenty-five years, during which time he has examined every piece of market literature that has been issued & procurable in Wall Street. It was he who encouraged Mr. Gann to study the scientific and mathematical possibilities of the subject. When asked what had been the most impressive of Mr. Gann's work and predictions, he replied as follows:

"It is very difficult for me to remember all the predictions and operations of W. D. Gann which may be classed as phenomenal, but the following are a few. "In 1908 when the Union Pacific was 168-1/8, he told me it would not touch 169 before it had a good break. We sold it short all the way down to 152-5/8, covering on the weak spots and putting it out again on the rallies, securing twenty-three points profit out of an eighteen-point market wave."

"He came to me when United States Steel was selling around 50, and said, "This steel will run up to 58 but it will not sell at 59. From there it should break 16 points." We sold it short around 58 with a stop at 59. The highest it went was 58. From there it declined to 41-17 points."

"At another time, wheat was selling at about 89¢. Gann predicted that the May option would sell at $1.35. We bought it and made large profits on the way up. It actually touched $1.35."

"When Union Pacific was 172, he said it would go to 184-7/8 but not an eighth higher until it had a good break. It went to 184-7/8 and came back from there eight or nine times. We sold it short repeatedly, with a stop at 185, and were never caught. It eventually came back to 17."

"Mr. Gann's calculations are based on natural law. I have followed Gann and his work closely for years. I know that he has a firm grasp of the basic principles which govern stock market movements, and I do not believe any other man can duplicate the idea or his method at the present time."

"Early this year, he figured that the top of the advance would fall on a certain day in August and calculated the prices at which the Dow Jones Averages would then stand. The market culminated on the exact day and within four-tenths of one percent of the figures predicted."

"You and W D Gann must have cleaned up considerable money on all these operations," was suggested.

"Yes, we have made a great deal of money. Gann has taken half-million dollars out of the market in the past few years. I once saw him take $130, and in less than one month run it up to over $12,000. Gann can compound money faster than any man I have ever met."

"One of the most astonishing calculations made by Mr. Gann was during last summer [1909] when he predicted that September Wheat would sell at $1.20. This meant that it must touch that figure before the end of the month of September. At twelve o'clock, Chicago time, on September 30th (the last day) the option was selling below $1.08, and it looked as though his prediction would not be fulfilled. Mr. Gann said, 'If it does not touch $1.20 by the close of the market it will prove that there is something wrong with my whole method of calculation. I do not care what the price is now, it must go there.' It is common history that September Wheat surprised the whole country by selling at $1.20 and no higher in the very last hour of trading, closing at that figure."

So much for what W D Gann has said and done as evidenced by him & others. Now as to what demonstrations have taken place before our representative:

During the month of October 1909, in twenty-five market days, W D Gann made, in the presence of our representative, two hundred and eighty-six transactions in various stocks, on both the long and short side of the market. Two hundred and sixty-four of these transactions resulted in profits; twenty-two in losses.

The capital with which he operated was doubled ten times, so that at the end of the month he had one thousand percent of his original margin.

In our presence Mr. William D. Gann sold Steel common short at 94-7/8, saying that it would not go to 95. It did not.

On a drive that occurred during the week ending October 29, Mr. Gann bought U.S. Steel common stock at 86-1/4, saying that it would not go to 86. The lowest it sold was 86-1/3.

We have seen Gann give in one day sixteen successive orders in the same stock, eight of which turned out to be at either the top or the bottom eighth of that particular swing. The above we can positively verify.

Such performances as these, coupled with the foregoing, are probably unparalleled in the history of the Street.

James R. Koene has said, "The man who is right six times out of ten will make a fortune." Gann is a trader who, without any attempt to make a showing, for he did not know the results were to be published, established a record of over ninety-two percent profitable trades.

Mr. W. D. Gann has refused to disclose his method at any price, but to those scientifically inclined he has unquestionably added to the stock of Wall Street knowledge and pointed out infinite possibilities.

We have requested Mr. Gann to figure out for the readers of the Ticker a few of the most striking indications, which appear in his calculations. In presenting these we wish it understood that no man, in or out of Wall Street, is infallible.

William D Gann's figures at present indicate that the trend of the stock market should, barring the usual rallies, be toward the lower prices until March or April 1910.

He calculates that May Wheat, which is now selling at $1.02, should not sell below 99 and should sell at $1.45 next spring.

On Cotton, which is now at about 15¢ level, he estimates that after a good reaction from these prices the commodity should reach 18 in the spring of 1910. He looks for a corner in the March or May option.

Whether these figures prove correct or not will in no way detract from the record which W. D. Gann has already established.

William Delbert Gann was born in Lufkin, Texas, and is thirty-one years of age. He is a gifted mathematician, has an extraordinary memory for figures, and is an expert Tape Reader. Take away his science and he would beat the market on his intuitive tape reading alone.

Endowed as he is with such qualities, we have no hesitation in predicting that, within a comparatively few years, William D. Gann will receive recognition as one of Wall Street's leading operators.

Note: Since the market forecast was made, Coffee has suffered the expected decline, the extreme break having been 120 points. The lowest on the May wheat thus far has been $1.01-5/8. It is now selling at $1.06-1/4.

It is very clear from this article that W. D. Gann knew exactly what he was doing. It's felt that Gann allowed this view of his trading and the article to be written so that he might be exposed to the public and so that they might understand that there were others ways of trading that were based on scientific methods rather than on the other methods known during the current day.

W.D. GANN A LEGEND by Les Clemens

Reproduced from Traders World Magazine

William Delbert Gann was born June 6, 1878, in Lufkin, Texas, to Sam H. and Susan R. Gann, immigrants to Texas from the British Isles. Lufkin is midway between Houston and Texarkana. This part of Texas is cotton country and Gann's parents lived on a Neches River bottom cotton ranch near Lufkin. He grew up around the cotton warehouses in Angelina County where cotton was king. W. D. Gann was raised in a very strict Methodist church family. His mother, a very religious person, encouraged him to read the Bible at a very early age, and in fact, wanted him to become a minister. Gann was not sure he wanted to become a minister, but studying the Bible was certainly easier than working in the cotton fields, as was his father's wish. He attended church every Sunday with his parents and as he listened to the sermons found his interpretation of the Bible scriptures to differ from the minister's. In the Bible he discovered time cycles, repetition of important numbers, and references to the wise men following the stars. Also, that it was written in veiled language that made interpreting the real meaning difficult. Since Gann had a photographic memory, by age 21 he had nearly memorized the Bible. During his school years Gann excelled in mathematics and was generally called as a gifted mathematician. His tremendous appetite for knowledge and his open-minded attitude led him into many different fields of study that eventually resulted in discoveries in the markets that would otherwise have been overlooked. He completed high school in a time when most children were only able to attend school through the third or fourth grade.

As a teenager, Gann liked to be called W. D., and he used these initials the rest of his life. W. D. pestered his parents until they relented and signed a minor release form that he needed to obtain a job. His first job was that of a News Butcher on the passenger train between Texarkana and Tyler, Texas. This job required him to be quick-witted, aggressive, and able to deal with all kinds of people. During his teen years, he worked in the cotton warehouses in Lufkin and Texarkana, Texas. While working in the cotton warehouse, he was introduced to commodity trading.

In 1902, at age 24, W. D. Gann made his first commodity trade in cotton, the market he knew best. The small profit from that trade marked the beginning of what was to become one of the most remarkable and legendary careers the speculative markets have ever known. Over the next 53 years, Gann took over $50,000,000 from the markets. It has been reported by a man who worked for Gann the last eight years of Gann's life, that approximately 1/3 of the money he made was for himself and the other 2/3 was for the accounts he supervised for clients. From that very first trade, it is believed Gann was using principles and techniques he continued using throughout his trading career. The notations on some of his early charts substantiated this belief. As time progressed, his trading methods were refined.

In 1906 W. D. went to Oklahoma City. He worked as a broker for a brokerage firm, trading for himself while handling large accounts for clients. He studied the cause of success and failure in the speculation of other traders. He found that over 90% of traders who enter the markets without knowledge and study usually lose in the end. Gann also lost a significant amount of money and admitted his trading was based on hope, greed, and fear. Later on, in his books and courses, he cautioned all traders about these emotions.

Early on, Gann began to note the periodical recurrence of rise and fall in stocks and commodities. This led him to conclude that natural law was the basis of market movements. He then devoted ten years to the study of natural law as applicable to the speculative markets. During that time he traveled to England, Egypt, and India to gain knowledge in ancient mathematics and astrology. In the British Museum in England he conducted extensive research on market cycles. In an Egyptian temple it is believed he found the basic construction of what was to become known as his Square of 9 Chart. After exhaustive research and investigation of the known sciences, he discovered the Law of Vibration enabled him to accurately determine the exact prices to which stocks or commodities would trade within a given time, and that each stock or commodity had its own rate of vibration.

At age 27, Gann was a well-known name in the Southwest. His views on the analysis of cotton prices were so well respected that a Texarkana newspaper, The Daily Texarkanian, ran a story on Gann's cotton predictions.

In 1908, at age 30, Gann moved to New York and opened his own brokerage office at 18 Broadway. He began testing his theories and techniques in the market. On August 8, 1908, he made one of his greatest mathematical discoveries for predicting the trend of stocks and commodities. This was "The Master Time Factor." Within a year, it became clear to others that his success was based on more than just luck. No one researched time cycles as extensively as Gann. His charts show the cycles with which he worked, went back to history's beginning, and bore no resemblance to other researcher's time cycle studies.

In October 1909, Richard D. Wyckoff, Owner and Editor of The Ticker and Investment Digest asked Gann for an interview to document his trading ability for one month. The interview was granted, and Gann's trades were monitored for 25 market days during the month of October in the presence of a Ticker representative. At that time the markets also traded on Saturday. Gann made 286 trades in various stocks, both long and short. There were 264 trades that resulted in profits and 22 in losses. 92.3% of the trades were profitable. The capital used doubled ten times resulting in 1000% gain on his original investment during those 25 trading days. What makes this even more phenomenal is that Gann did this with an average time between each trade of about twenty minutes. In one day Gann made 16 trades in the same stock, 8 of which were in either the top eighth or the bottom eighth of that particular swing. Such a performance is unparalleled in the history of Wall Street. As stated by James R. Keene, the famous speculator of that era, "The man who is right 6 times out of 10 will make his fortune."

It seems a foregone conclusion that Gann was picking tops and bottoms with a high degree of accuracy. At this point of time, in 1909, he was only 31 years of age, so whatever methods he was using had already been discovered.

This biographer believes that after his sensational performance

Gann regretted having granted the interview, as it was stated in the printed article that he did not know the results were to be published. When the article was printed in The Ticker Investment Digest, Gann was besieged with people asking how he was able to pick tops and bottoms as he had demonstrated. His only answer to them was he used The Law of Vibration to make all his calculations. At this conjuncture there were only two choices: 1) to give away his secret discoveries and risk destroying the markets, or 2) to detract from his method of picking tops and bottoms by writing books and courses about mechanical trading systems, the use of geometrical angles, the use of Time and Price Charts, such as the Octagon Chart (Square of 9), Master 12 Chart (Square of 144), Hexagon Chart (the cube), Square of 90, Square of 52, 360 Degree Circle Chart, and many other trading techniques.

If Gann had continued trading using only his method of picking tops and bottoms, without a doubt he would have become one of the wealthiest men in the world, and in so doing would have attracted too much attention. He would have been asked too many questions by traders and would have been compelled to explain. However, at certain times, he probably used his method to advantage. Gann had a profound understanding of natural law, so rather than place himself in an embarrassing situation, he chose to trade using his mechanical systems and other techniques he had developed. Also, having more capital than was required for a good living was not important to him, as he was more interested in the knowledge possessed by ancient civilizations and the occult sciences. Gann understood how the Laws of Nature controlled human beings and, therefore, he understood the markets, because the markets are nothing more than an expression of the actions of human beings.

The two previous paragraphs are my belief. You may agree or disagree, but before you arrive at a conclusion, carefully study Gann's 1909 trading demonstration. He made 286 trades in 25 days, which is 11 trades per day. To do this, you must pick the tops and bottoms on a short intraday time period.

If what I believe is true, it is very sad to think that a genius individual such as W. D. Gann, had to disguise the truth throughout his life, with a smoke screen of many trading methods and techniques.

In 1918 his office address in New York was 81 New Street and in the early 1920's was at 49 Broadway. Over the years, Gann maintained several offices in New York all located on Wall Street with the address numbers of 78, 80, 82, 88, 91, 93 and 99.

At the height of Gann's career, he employed 35 individuals who made charts of all kinds, did analytical research at his direction, and performed many duties involved with his various publications and services. The name of one of his businesses was W. D. Gann Scientific Service, Inc., and the other, initiated in 1919, was W. D. Gann Research, Inc.

The firms published the following Supply and Demand Letters: Daily Stock Letter, Tri-Weekly Stock Letter, Weekly Stock Letter, Daily Commodity Letter, Tri-Weekly Commodity Letter, and Weekly Commodity Letter. Telegraph Service was all offered as follows: Daily Telegraph Service on Stocks, Daily Telegraph Service on Cotton, Daily Telegraph Service on Grain, and Telegrams on important Changes Only, on Stocks or Commodities. Published under Annual Forecasts were: Annual Stock Forecast, Annual Cotton Forecast, Annual Grain Forecast, Annual Rubber Forecast, Annual Coffee, Sugar and Cocoa Forecast. Supplements to all Forecasts were issued and mailed on the first of each month. Special Forecasts on stocks or other commodities were made on request. Also offered were daily, weekly, monthly, quarterly, and swing charts on stocks and commodities. Gann taught advanced courses of instruction entitled Master Forecasting Method, at a cost of $2,500, and New Mechanical Method and Trend Indicator, at a cost of $5,000, to those who want it for their own use and will not publish, sell, or teach it to others. It is too valuable to be spread broadcasted. The cost of these courses and personal instruction in today's economics would be $25,000 to $50,000, or more.

As early as 1923, Gann offered a service entitled "The Busy-Man's Service." This was a service for professional and businessmen where Gann supervised their trading accounts by advising them what and when to buy and sell. In later years the name of this service was changed to "Personal Service." The cost of this service was on a 1-month, 3-months, 6-months, or annual basis, or on a Part-of-Profit Plan where the monthly fee was smaller and Gann received 5% of the net profits. Under the Part-of-Profit Plan it was required that a minimum of 100 shares be traded. The clients were advised by telegram or letter. An article in The Evening Telegram dated New York, Monday, March 5, 1923, used the words "prophet" and "mathematical seer" to describe Gann. It also stated his followers declared he was 85% correct in his forecasts. He predicted the election of Wilson and Harding using fortunate numbers and fortunate letters combined with cycles. He predicted the abdication of the Kaiser and the end of the war to the exact date six months in advance. His predictions were based on mathematics. He stated if he had the data he would use algebra and geometry to tell exactly by the theory of cycles when a certain thing is going to occur again. He further stated that there is no chance in nature, because mathematical principles of the highest order lie at the foundation of all things. The article pointed out that Gann received calls every day from prominent persons asking him to cast their horoscope. It also said he told politicians whether or not they would be elected and solved problems for clergymen, bankers, and statesmen.

In another article in the Morning Telegraph, dated Sunday, December 17, 1922, the Financial Editor, Arthur Angy, stated that "W. D. Gann had scored another astounding hit in his 1922 stock forecast issued in December, 1921, I found his 1921 forecast so remarkable that I secured a copy of his 1922 stock forecast to prove his claims for myself. And now, at the closing of the current year of 1922, it is but justice to say I am more than amazed by the result of Mr. Gann's remarkable predictions based on pure science and mathematical calculations."

W. D. and his wife, Sadie H. Gann, had one son and three daughters born to their marriage. Their son, John L. Gann, was in partnership with his father for several years in the late 1930's and early 1940's, operating under the firm name of W. D. Gann & Son, Inc. Apparently, the two personalities were not always compatible, as their association was ended in the mid 1940's. This writer has been told one of their main differences concerned astrology, as John did not believe astrology had any effect on market movements, or human behavior. This probably upset W. D. as he knew well the effect of planetary motion on the markets and the individual. Following the association with his father, John served as a broker for many years for the firm Sulzbacher, Granger & Co. in New York City. It is believed that John passed away in 1984.

For many years Gann maintained a home in Scarsdale, New York, which was, at the time, the estate bedroom community for New York City. In an article that appeared in the May 26, 1933 New York Daily Investment News, it was reported that Gann left New York in the first 1933 model Stinson Reliant airplane, piloted by Flinor Smith, a woman aviator, to conduct an extensive tour of the country analyzing cotton, wheat, and tobacco crops, and business conditions. The airplane was equipped with navigation instruments, radio receiving equipment and extra-large fuel tanks that gave a flying range of 750 miles. It was powered with a Lycoming engine and cruised at 135 miles per hour. Gann was the first Wall Street advisor to use an airplane for studying market conditions so he could advise clients much faster of changing market conditions. During his trip he was a speaker to members of Kiwanis, Rotary, Chamber of Commerce, and other business organizations in various larger cities throughout the United States.

In 1935, Gann made an airplane trip to South America for studying crop conditions, and to gather information on the increase and production of cotton in Peru, Chili, Argentina, and Brazil. He logged 18,000 miles by air and another 1,000 miles by automobile. In July of 1936 Gann purchased a specially built all metal airplane, which he named "The Silver Star," and used in making crop surveys. In July of 1939 he purchased a new Fairchild airplane for the same purpose.

Gann was a member of the Commodity Exchange, Inc. of New York, the New Orleans Cotton Exchange, the Rubber Exchange of New York, the Royal Economic Society of London, the American Economic Society, the Masonic Lodge, the Shrine, the Chicago Board of Trade, and was a devout Christian in the Methodist Church.

Gann had a winter home in Miami, Florida, and in the 1940's moved there on a full-time basis. His office was at 820 S. W. 26th

Road in Miami. While in Florida, he continued his advisory services as well as teaching his commodity and stock market courses, either in person or by mail. By the late 1940's he had a recommended list of Books For Sale that included the subjects of numerology, astrology, scientific, and miscellaneous. He was involved in real estate holdings, and enjoyed large automobiles, especially Lincolns, which he purchased new yearly. In 1954, after making several successful coffee and soybean trades, Gann purchased a fast express cruising boat that he named "The Coffee Bean." It was reported that Gann wore the same type of suit throughout his life, and that his home was filled with items collected in his world travels. He vacationed often in South America. But, in the opinion of his peers, he did not live beyond his means.

W. D. Gann wrote some of the best books ever written on the stock and commodity markets. The following is a list of the books written by him and the year they were published:

Speculation a Profitable Profession

The Truth of the Stock Tape

The Tunnel Thru the Air

Wall Street Stock Selector

Stock Trend Detector Scientific Stock Forecasting

How to Make Profits Trading in Puts and Calls

Face Facts America. Looking Ahead to 1950

How to Make Profits Trading in Commodities

45 Years in Wall Street

The Magic Word

How to Make Profits Trading in Commodities

Gann was a prolific writer. His style of writing was unique. Readers of his books considered him to be a poor writer with a limited use of the English language. Not so! Upon methodic study of his work, the reader will discover in time the Gann method of teaching. He will inspire the reader to research everything from the origin of numbers to the musical scale and vibrations.

W. D. Gann, in my estimation, was a genius. He was born a Gemini with a high intellectual capacity, and a dual personality that caused him to be both genial and obstinate. He was a gifted mathematician, an expert chart reader, and had an extraordinary memory for figures. Take away his science and he would beat the market on chart reading alone. One of Gann's most important technical tools was his charts and no one kept up as many as he did. Gann's charts encompassed 55 years, from 1900 to 1955. During this time thousands of daily, weekly, monthly, quarterly, yearly, and other various charts, were made with great care, each a work of art. He believed charting was an art and if you understood everything the chart was showing, it would aid in forecasting the next day, week, or month's, price movements. Gann was a workaholic, at times working 17 hours per day, 6 days per week. He was very demanding of those who worked with and for him, and expected the same effort from them that he himself put forth. He expected to issue instructions only once and did not feel it should be necessary to repeat them.

Gann was deeply analytical and studied price actions of various stocks and commodities back through the years. He spent nine months in the British Museum working day and night researching stock and commodity prices and dates from 1820, and wheat prices and dates from 1200. He also spent long hours and long days in the Astor Library in New York City researching stock and commodity markets. He was a student of numbers, number theory, progressions, and the progression of numbers. His trading system was based on natural law and mathematics. Since time progresses as the earth rotates on its axis and in its order, and time is measured by numbers and progression of numbers, and prices in their movement upward and downward are also measured in numbers, it is understandable why Gann had an intense interest in numbers, number theory, and mathematics. A keen understanding of natural laws and their effect on mankind have a direct effect on the markets. The markets are only extensions or reflections of man's actions.

In Gann's time there were no calculators. He used a slide rule and the various master charts he developed, such as the Square of 9, for his calculator. He kept an open mind to any trading ideas to achieve perfection. When making his forecasts, he used many methods to arrive at the time for a trend change, and all of them to confirm he was correct. In his early trading he made thousands of dollars. But, by listening to false rumors and other people's ideas, he also lost thousands of dollars. In 1913 and again in 1919, he lost small fortunes when the brokerage firms he was trading with went bankrupt. One of these firms was Murray Mitchell and Company. In those days the client's funds were not protected by exchange regulations in case of a failure, as they are today. During this time he was also involved in two bank failures. Regardless of these losses and misfortunes, he was always able to rely upon mathematical science to aid him in making a financial comeback. This is why Gann states that knowledge of the market is more important than money.

Today, people believe "times are different," but Gann's time saw its bull markets and panics in the stock market, bull markets and panics, in the commodity market, wars, inflationary periods, depressions, bank closings, etc. In 1921 the rate of inflation was 100%. Strikes were rampant, jobs impossible to find, and productivity at very low levels. The Great Depression of 1929 to 1932 and the outright confiscation of the citizen's gold that was exchanged for printed money, left deep scars on the country and its citizens. W. D. Gann was avidly against the New Deal and Roosevelt's creeping socialism. Therefore, to learn from other people's past experiences, people today should understand Gann's famous quotation, "The future is but a repetition of the past, or as the Bible says, the thing that hath been, it is that which shall be; and that which is done, is that which shall be done; and there is no new thing under the Sun." Gann said, "The average man's memory is too short. He only remembers what he wants to remember or what suits his hopes and fears. He depends too much on others and does not think for himself. Therefore, he should keep a record, graph, or picture of past market movements to remind him what has happened in the past can, and will, happen in the future. Panics will come and bull markets will follow just as long as the world stands and they are just as sure as the ebb and flow of the tides, because it is the nature of man to overdo everything. He goes to the extreme when he gets hopeful and optimistic. When fear takes hold of him, he goes to the extreme in the other direction."

The following is taken from 45 Years in Wall Street and is very good advice and very true in today's world. "Every man takes out of life just exactly according to what he puts in. We reap just what we sow. A man who pays with time and money for knowledge and continues to study and never gets to the point where he thinks he knows all there is to know, but realizes that he can still learn, is the man who will make a success in speculation or in investments. I am trying to tell you the truth and give you the benefit of over 45 years of operating in stocks and commodities markets and point out to you the weak points that will prevent you from meeting with disaster. Speculation can be made a profitable profession. Wall Street can be beaten and there is money operating in commodities and the stock market if you follow the rules and always realize that the unexpected can happen and be prepared for it."

In How to Make Profits in Commodities -- Gann made the following comments regarding knowledge as he believed knowledge is power. All who read this should heed and always remember his advice. "The difference between success and failure in trading in commodities is the difference between one man knowing and following fixed rules and the other man guessing. The man who guesses usually loses. Therefore, if you want to make a success and make profits, your object must be to know more; study all the time; never think that you know it all. I have been studying stocks and commodities for forty years, and I do not know it all yet. I expect to continue to learn something every year as long as I live. Observations, and keen comparisons of past market movements, will reveal what commodities are going to do in the future, because the future is but a repetition of the past. Time spent in gaining knowledge is money in the bank. You can lose all the money you may accumulate or that you may inherit - that is if you have no knowledge of how to take care of it - but with knowledge you can take a small amount of money and make more after time spent in gaining knowledge. A study of commodities will return rich rewards."

Sometime in 1947, Gann sold W. D. Gann Research, Inc. to C. C. Loosli, a San Francisco attorney. He became disenchanted with the business and on February 14, 1948, W. D. Gann Research, Inc. was transferred to Mr. Joseph L. Lederer of St. Louis, Missouri. The office for W. D. Gann Research, Inc. was maintained at 82 Wall Street in New York until 1952. Then it was moved to Scarsdale, New York, and in 1956 relocated to St. Louis, Missouri, where its only business was that of investment adviser.

In 1950 in Miami, Florida, Gann and a partner, Ed Lambert, founded Lambert-Gann Publishing Co. Ed Lambert was an architect who designed the Inter-State Highway System in the greater Miami area Lambert Gann Publishing Co. published all Gann's books and courses.

W. D. Gann passed away in the Methodist Hospital in Brooklyn, New York, on June 14, 1955, at the age of 77. He was survived by his wife, Sadie, three daughters, and a son. That day the world truly lost a market legend.

After Mr. Gann's death in 1955, Ed Lambert continued to operate the business that included a chart service of updated Gann style charts. He was not as active in promoting Gann's writings as when Gann was alive, so for the following twenty years Gann's work became quite obscure. In 1976 Bill and Nikki Jones of Pomeroy, Washington, purchased Lambert-Gann Publishing Co. and the Gann copyrights. In the purchase were all of his personal research including thousands of his charts, papers, books, and writings he had collected through fifty years of trading and research. There were also tables and miscellaneous office furniture used by Gann. The largest Mayflower moving van available was required to transport this purchase to Pomeroy, Washington. Following

Billy Jones' death in September 1989, Nikki Jones continues to operate Lambert Gann Publishing Co., carrying on the Gann tradition with the sale of his books and courses. In this biographer's opinion, W. D. Gann was the greatest market researcher of all time. His trading career spanned more than a half century. During that time he devoted his total life to market research and trading. He researched every possible aspect of natural laws in conjunction with variables of price and time in market movements. This study became an obsession to find the cause and effect of market fluctuations, which he did. The trading techniques Gann developed work the same today as they did when he used them. His library contained volumes of books and manuscripts on harmonic waves, proportion, growth, gravity, electricity, nature, and natural phenomena. However, there were no books on open interest, volume, stocks, or commodities.

The only books and courses on commodities and stocks were his own. He was a humble man who stated, at age 75, that he had not learned all there was to know, and yet, he knew more about the markets than any trader who ever lived. There is an important lesson to be learned from the study of his life and his work. For those of you who have diligently studied his writings, you will understand my statements. Hopefully, for those of you who are not familiar with Gann, this writing will inspire you to begin.

COMPUTER

It's very important that you have the right kind of equipment to effectively trade real-time. Today it's recommended that you have at least an i5 and i7 computer using a highly reliable operating system like Windows 7 or 8. These operating systems are based on Microsoft's new systems, which have completely replaced the old DOS kernel systems. You should completely avoid Windows 95, 98 and Millennium systems. They are prone to constant breakdowns and lockups and should not be considered in the critical real-time atmosphere.

Screens

If you are a day-trader or even a regular investor then you should have at least one big 21-23" inch computer screens or multiple monitors. Some traders feel that one big monitor is easier to work with than multiple monitors. If you can put all of your charts, news, chat rooms and order execution programs on one monitor it might work for you. You can keep your eyes on one monitor and not have to look back and forth at several monitors.

COMPUTER CHAIR

Many people day-trade sitting in front of a computer hours and hours a day. The trader's chair is a very important piece of equipment and needs to be selected with care.

Most traders just go out to the their local discount store and buy the $99.00 secretary special. Others buy an executive plush chair at an office supply store. They think that the more they pay for the chair, the more comfortable it will be. The fact is that both of these chairs are at the extremes and neither are what a day-trader needs.

I have studied the motions of the average day-trader. He leans forward to answer a phone or study a chart or use the mouse. He leans back to chat or sits up at the keyboard to type. He swivels around to look-up a research book. The trader needs a chair, which automatically adjust to his movements and gives him constant back support.

Hector Serber, President of the American Ergonomics Corporation dedicated the past 15 years of his life developing seating products. He has been awarded numerous US and foreign patents for his work, and has been cited in such publications as the New York Times, Fortune and Business Week. His research led to the discoveries, which he has incorporated in a new office task chair called the Swing Seat. This chair seems to have all the right features for the day-trader. It adjusts in height, depth and angle of seat and back. Once the trader adjusts the chair to fit his body, its "smart motion" is automatic. It supports him dynamically as he moves through the many-seated tasks that he does each day.

The chair's movement is effortless. The secret is the Swing Seat's suspension system that adjusts from the trader's center of gravity. It's always balanced, the seat and back magically follows the trader. The chair's "smart motion" provides just the right amount of support and movement, whether the trader weighs 100 pounds or 250 pounds. I have never seen any other office chair that can support the trader's many postures so easily.

PSYCHOLOGY OF TRADING

There are some traders who are naturals at trading. W.D. Gann was one of them. These traders seem to thrive in the risky trading environment. They have the emotional capability of riding out the highs and lows of a market. They have the ability of being able to survive failures and continue onward. Traders constantly must face failures again and again. Some people simply are not capable of handling this. A good trader must have the ability of getting his mind into a state of trading performance. This state of mind should be based on motivation and recuperating from failure. The successful trader must be able to remake the frame of mind he was in when he did prior successful trading. By doing this he can bolster his self-assurance which should increase his success in trading.

Getting yourself into the right frame of mind is extremely important to your success. You must have the know how of how to do it. It's basically psychological. It's a matter of being totally focused, centered and everything is working. To be successful you must have the necessary tools that work, research, ideas and judgment. You will not necessarily be successful in all your trades when you're in the right frame of mind, but you substantially increase your capacity for success.

Being the right frame of mind for trading means that you have to have total self-control and concentration. You must have the ability to recover from failed trades to keep going with your successful momentum. It means continuing to do all the things you are supposed to do even after failure. You must have a strong degree of energy and keenness. You must have a far-reaching purpose and not just a short-term one.

Trading is an extremely complex practice because of the emotions triggered in the incredible instability and unpredictable nature of the market. Both day- traders and regular traders of the market experience this. There are emotional mental swings created by the wild up and down markets and these swings can cause you to change the way to trade from a successful pattern to an unsuccessful one. These changes may cause you to deviate from your trading plan and therefore cause you to lose money. This intern may cause you to go into state of mind of negative ness, which will interfere with your successful trading process. This can then give you the biggest problems with trading including fear of failure, a defensive behavior syndrome, and even a negative mindset, which can lead to be self-fulfilling to breakdown of your entire plan of success. This intern leads to anxiety and to poor judgment. It causes you to hold back on good trades and take bad trades. It also causes you to get out of winning trades too fast and to keep losing trades too long. The trader then will lose more money on the losing trade that he holds and the winning trade he gets out of too soon. This in a losing type of a cycle when you can no longer differential good trades by bad traders any longer, which complete destroys your program. Anxiety over the loosing trading causes the cycle to continue until the trader loses all hope and is devastated.

To be a successful trader like W.D. Gann was one must recognize the recurring patterns in their activities and the prior situation where they have been very successful. There are many forces that the trader can't understand at work here. A trader must try to put himself in the successful mindset and he can be better able to process information into successful actions. He must be capable of not letting hope or fear alter any of the decisions he makes.

It's hard to believe, must most successful Gann trades make the most of the money only on about 10% of their trades. The other 90% are stopped out with a small loss or marginal gain. That means that most of their trades are not making money. To trade successfully you need to learn the application of trading rules, intelligence, the ability to communicate and read what is important in the news and keeping frequently notes on what you are doing and improving your methods. This allows you to face your failures and successes and how to possibly change the failures into possible futures successes. When you find something that is really working you need to be able to double up. When you find something that is not working right you need to be able to get out of it immediately and not look back. Keep your mind open free from fears, doubts and previous mistakes.

The virtual ease of entry into day-trading on the internet has caused many inexperienced traders to start trading this way. Data is easily available. Charting software programs are available everywhere. Fundamental information is accessible from many sites. You must learn how to learn how to process and trading the information available on the Internet. You must have a proven method or way of assimilating this information and putting it into a successful trading program. It is usually necessary for the new trader to paper trade for many months until he is confident to trade with real money. Some traders need to have a mentor who can help them get started in the right way.

THE RIGHT KIND OF CHARTS

It's very important to have the right kind of charts to follow stocks or commodities. The major problem with most traders is, they do not have the right kind of charts to study the market correctly. If you talk to a carpenter or a surgeon or any professional person, they will tell you the importance of having the necessary tools to get the job done right. Can you imagine a surgeon operating on a patient with a dull scalpel or a carpenter using a dull saw? We'll that's precisely what a trader is doing when he trades with most of today's published chart services. Traders risk thousands of dollars trading with ineffective tools. If you are going to build a house, it is very important to build it on a strong foundation. To start trading according to the rules of W. D. Gann you must have the right foundation, and that's a proper and correct chart.

Bar Charts

Bar charts are the type of charts that you should set up. They should be set up correctly according to price and time. They must be set up either on a high, low, close basis or on an open, high, low close basis. It is necessary that you have enough update space so you can project out future points of time and price. The update space should be labeled out in the future with the year, month and day's date. This is another thing that is very wrong with most chart services they don't put enough update space out to the right of the chart so you can the proper projecting of prices. On a daily chart you should have at least 1 year of update space, a weekly chart should have 2-3 years and a monthly chart should have 3-5 years of update space.

Holidays

A holiday on a daily chart must be omitted (do no leave a space for it). When you are projecting out into the future you must be aware of when the holidays occur so you can adjust your charts for them. Usually toward the end of the prior year, around November to December most brokerage firms and some financial magazines will publish the dates that the exchanges are closed on.

There has been much discussion regarding the type of charts to keep. Should you keep a regular Gann type charts, which omits weekends and holidays? This type of chart plots only market days. Or, should you keep up a calendar day bar chart. This type of chart leaves blank spaces for both holidays and weekends when the market did not trade. The answer to this important question is that it takes too much time to keep both types of charts up. You should only keep up Gann style charts and use the Excel spreadsheet for calendar day-time counts. You do need to be aware of both calendar and market day timing. When a market makes a high it will bottom out a set number of market trading days and calendar days out in the future. Time counts will be discussed in a later chapter.

Market Reports

It's very important to mark on the update space on your charts the market reports that directly affect your commodity or stock. For example, if you are trading cattle, you would mark on the update space the dates of all the cattle-on-feed reports. You also need to mark the quarterly pig reports on the chart as they affect cattle prices. The grain reports have some influence on cattle prices, so they should also be marked on the charts also. Often important projected highs or lows will occur on the day after a market report. If you have several important cycles hitting near a major report day, then probably the day after the report day will be the timing or reversal day. Most important reports come after the market closes. That's why we say the day after the report will be the timing day. If the report is during the trading hours of the commodity or stock, then that day will probably be the timing day.

Moon and Sun Cycles

It's also very important to mark on the update space on your charts the days that full or new moons and Sun Ellipses occur. Many major pivot points in the markets occur during these cycle times of the sun and moon.

Important Future Months

A good set of charts should include the key months of future contracts of the year in commodity future contracts. For example, in most commodities the 12th and 6th positions of the cycle (December and June) are the most important and the 3rd and 9th positions (March and October) are the second most important. You should keep charts on all four of the important months, if you are trading actively.

Proper Scale

The proper scale is very important. The correct scale can be determined from how plastic overlays fit the charts. You will learn about overlays in a later chapter. The master time and price overlays were one of the most significant discoveries W.D. Gann ever made. He said that himself before he died. To determine if your overlays are working properly, the 1 x 1 angle on the overlays should usually hit the 50% reaction of prices and bounce off at least the first time. Once you see this on many charts you will understand the principal. The scaling is also very important. The rule in commodities is to use the following order in scaling.

DECIMAL commodities	FRACTION commodities
.10	1 cents
.20	2 cents
.40	4 cents
.80	8 cents
1.00	10 cents

Time Format

The charts you use should be correctly formatted into the right time format to be effective for trading. We recommend using charts going back 20 - 100 years in the following time formats:

Daily

Weekly Monthly Yearly

For intraday charts you should use the following time formats:

60 Minute 30 Minute 15 Minute

5 Minute

2 Minute

1 Minute

Linking Contracts Together

In using Gann Style charts it is necessary to link the contracts together correctly. The procedure for linking contracts together is very simple and is necessary for the proper continuation of the time series of prices.

Daily

For the current contract, for example, December 1990 corn, plot all the prices to the end of the contract including the last trading day. Then start with the next contract, 1991 corn and start plotting those prices in sequence till the end of the 1991 contract then start with the 1992 contract. Always use the same month of contracts linking them together, for example Dec. 1989, Dec. 1990, Dec. 1991 and so on.

Weekly

For weekly charts plot all the daily prices inside the weekly to the end of the contract. For example if the trading on a commodity like Dec. 1990 corn stopped in the middle of the week, stop there and continue the daily prices on the Dec. 1991 contract in that same weekly price bar.

Monthly

For monthly charts plot all the daily prices inside the monthly to the end of the contract. For example if the trading on a commodity like Dec. 1990 corn stopped in the middle of the month, stop there and continue the daily prices on the Dec. 1991 contract in that same monthly price bar.

Yearly

For yearly charts plot all the daily prices inside the yearly to the end of the contract. For example, if the trading on a commodity like Dec. 1990 corn stopped in the middle of the year, stop there and continue the daily prices on the Dec. 1991 contract in that same yearly price bar.

Continuous

Many people use a type of chart called a continuous contract chart. These are the type of weekly charts that are in almost of the chart services. In this type of contract all the nearby months of a commodity are linked together, for example, Dec. 1990 corn, Mar. 1990 corn, Jun. 1990 corn and so on. It's OK to use this type of chart to find rough cycles with using an Ehrlich Cycle Finder, but they are not very good for projecting accurate price and cycle projections according to the rules of W.D. Gann.

Time and Price Labels

The time and price labels at the bottom of the chart are very important. The date bar should be correctly labeled at the bottom of the chart showing year, month and day. The prices should be correctly labeled on the side with price divisions in circle numbers if possible. Circle numbers will be explained in another chapter.

Chart Services

The availability of good charts is hard to come by. Most chart services do not give you daily prices that go back far enough. They usually give you only about 6-7 months of daily data. That is not enough to do long term research necessary for Gann trading. You should have at least 3 years of daily data linked together according to the methods of W.D. Gann. The weekly and monthly charts they put out are nearby continuous charts that cannot be used correctly due to incorrect highs and lows.

Doing charts by hand

Making and keeping up charts by hand is very time consuming, but it does give you a special feel of the market that you would not otherwise get having prices updated automatically in a chart service or computer. If you feel that you have the necessary time for this activity, then the chart paper and printed data can be ordered from Gann Masters.

Computer charts

You can also buy a computer and obtain charting software to do precision charts. GannTrader 3.0, Market-Analyst and Ensign Software are programs, which adhere to the correct Gann proportion in charting. The only real-time program right now is Ensign software, which is highly acclaimed by its users. Ensign for Windows has been around for a long time and it's extremely stable. It performs Gann real time trading functions better in any software out there. Many suggestions by subscribers have been programmed into the program by its excellent the technical staff of Ensign software. A real working demo of this software is available on the CD in the back of this book and with the demo data used in this book for illustrations. With this software and data you can experiment with all of the techniques given in this book.

Ensign for Windows works through two major data vendors, eSignal and DTN. The software we used for this book was eSignal version 6.1. The main advantage of eSignal is that with Ensign for Windows you have access to the online database of historical data. This means you never have to worry about updating your database in your computer. Before now you had to constantly have your computer on downloading every tick into your computer. If your computer went down for some reason you lost ticks and had a gap in your data, which was a disaster. Now all the problems have been eliminated with the real time eSignal online database.

This database in available in different time frames: 1, 2, 3, 5, 10, 15, 20, 30, 45, 60, TICK, Daily, Weekly and Monthly.

The best time cycles to use are the ones that are based on the circle of 360°. Therefore the Daily, Weekly and Monthly cycles all based on the 365 days of the year are excellent. All the intraday time frames of 1, 2, 3, 5, 10, 15, 20, 30, 45 and 60 can be used as a divider of the circle of 360 and are valid. You will find many of the intraday cycles are more easily followed using the 30 and 60-minute bars. Once you find the pattern or cycle the market is working in you can then break it down into the smaller time frames. The most logical breakdown of time frames would be 60, 30, 15, 5, 2, 1 and the tick chart.

One of the theories of Gann analysis is that if your method of trading is valid, that it must work in any time frame. In the following pages you find that theory to be true. There are the big, medium, small and minute cycles in the market. All of these cycles work together. One cycles is a part of every other cycle. Trend lines work with each and every wave, as do all valid indicators used by technicians. If you find an indicator or method that works only part of the time, then it probably is not valid and should not be used.

It's very important that you work with the main trend of the market. To find the main trend of the market you need to look at the big picture. That means looking at Monthly, weekly and daily charts. You can't do it along with intraday charts, even though Ensign for Windows has done an outstanding job with these charts.

TRADING SOFTWARE

To effectively trade the market in real time you need real time analytical charting software, which works through the Internet. In this book we chose Ensign Software for Windows, which is the most effective real time Gann trading software on the market currently. Ensign for Windows has been around for a long time and it's extremely stable. It performs Gann real time trading functions better in any software out there. Many suggestions by subscribers have been programmed into the program by its excellent the technical staff of Ensign Software. A real working demo of this software is available on the CD in the back of this book and with the demo data used in this book for illustrations. With this software and data you can experiment with all of the techniques given in this book.

Ensign for Windows works through two major data vendors, eSignal and DTN. The software we used for this book was eSignal version 6.1. The main advantage of eSignal is that with Ensign for Windows you have access to the online database of historical data. This means you never have to worry about updating your database in your computer. Before now you had to constantly have your computer on downloading every tick into your computer. If your computer went down for some reason you lost ticks and had a gap in your data, which was a disaster. Now all the problems have been eliminated with the real time eSignal online database.

This database in available in different time frames:

1, 2, 3, 5, 10, 15, 20, 30, 45, 60, TICK, Daily, Weekly, Monthly

The best time cycles to use are the ones that are based on the circle of 360°. Therefore the Daily, Weekly and Monthly cycles all based on the 365 days of the year are excellent. All the intraday time frames of 1, 2, 3, 5, 10, 15, 20, 30, 45 and 60 can be used as a divider of the circle of 360 and are valid. You will find many of the intraday cycles are more easily followed using the 30 and 60-minute bars. Once you find the pattern or cycle the market is working in you can then break it down into the smaller time frames. The most logical breakdown of time frames would be 60,

30, 15, 5, 2, 1 and the tick chart.

One of the theories of Gann analysis is that if your method of trading is valid, that it must work in any time frame. In the following pages you find that theory to be true. There are the big, medium, small and minute cycles in the market. All of these cycles work together. One cycles is a part of every other cycle. Trend lines work with each and every wave, as do all valid indicators used by technicians. If you find an indicator or method that works only part of the time, then it probably is not valid and should not be used.

It's very important that you work with the main trend of the market. To find the main trend of the market you need to look at the big picture. That means looking at Monthly, weekly and daily charts. You can't do it along with intraday charts, even though Ensign for Windows has done an outstanding job with these charts.

INTRADAY TREND – PRICE ACTION

The market can basically be in three different trends.

1) Uptrend

2) Downtrend

3) Sideways

It's important that you know the market trend. You first need to look at the long-term trend (monthly charts), then the intermediate trend (weekly charts) and then the short-term trend (daily charts). Then for day trading you look at another 3 trends, the 5-minute, 15-minute and the 30 or 60-minute chart.

TO BUY

If the long-term trend is up, wait for the intermediate trend (weekly charts) to break up out of a long running consolidation and then buy after the first short-term (daily charts) drop turns up. Then on the intraday charts make sure the 30-minute charts are in a rising trend. Wait for the 15-minute charts breakout from a running consolidation and then buy the 5-minute chart after it turns up from a correction.

TO SELL

To sell you do the opposite of the buy. Make sure the long-term trend is down. Wait for the intermediate trend (weekly charts) to break down out of a long running consolidation and then sell after the first short-term (daily charts) uptrend turns down. Then on the intraday charts make sure the 30-minute charts are in a downtrend. Wait for the 15-minute charts breakout from a running consolidation then sell the 5-minute chart after it urns up from a correction.

In most cases you can just look at the intra-day charts to get a handle on the trend of the day for day-trading. Just look at the 30 or 6- minute chart and determine the main trend of the day. Then look at the 15-minute chart and wait for a breakout of a consolidation. Then used a small correction on the 5-minute chart to enter the market. See the following examples of the following chart.

In situations like this you can put your trade on with a very low risk. Close stops can be used for protection. You should always take your positions when the 30 or 6- minute charts are making

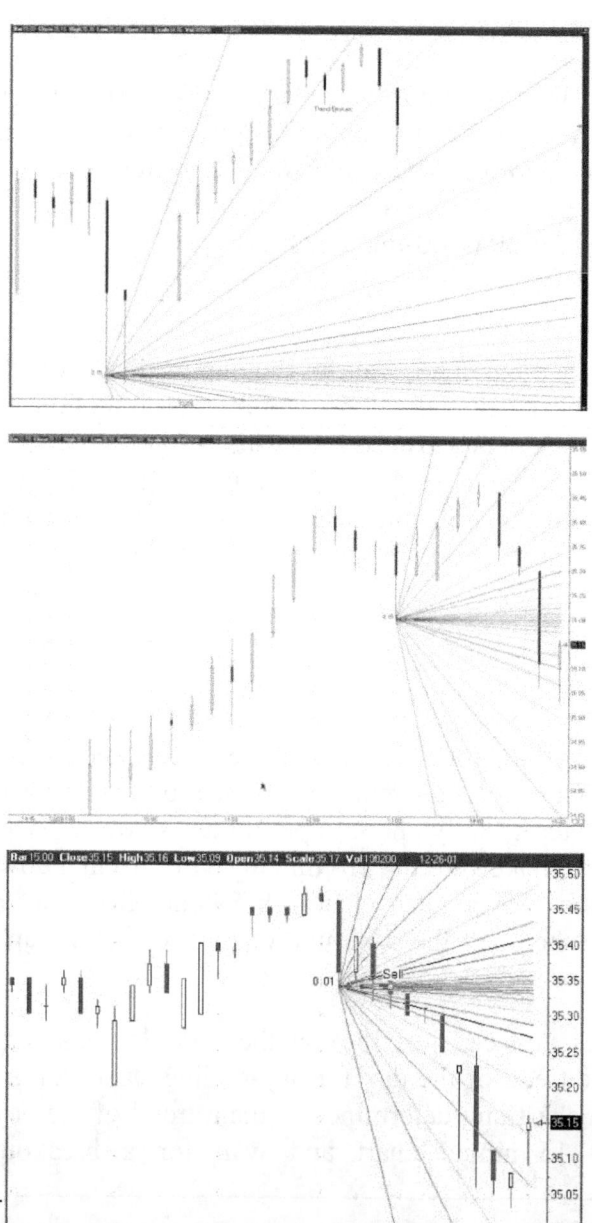

new highs or lows. Wait for the first reaction of the 15-minute chart and then enter the market with the 5-minute chart breaks out.

INTRADAY TRENDS – TIME ACTION

The time factor is extremely important in showing a change in trend. When the trend of an intraday market makes a trend the number of units of reaction will increase over the last reaction. This is one of the first indications of a change in trend. First for the main trend you need to keep an eye on the number of days reaction on the long term charts which, of course, is the daily, weekly and monthly charts. On the daily charts watch both the calendar days and trading days reactions. On calendar days watch all the trading days including both the weekends and holidays. On trading days watch only the trading days. Also keep an eye on the number of units of reaction in the 60 or 30-minute chart, the 15-minute chart and the 5-minute chart.

Here is an example of overbalance of time. You see the first two rallies stopped at B in time. The third rally again stopped at B, but finally went through it changing the direction of the market in time.

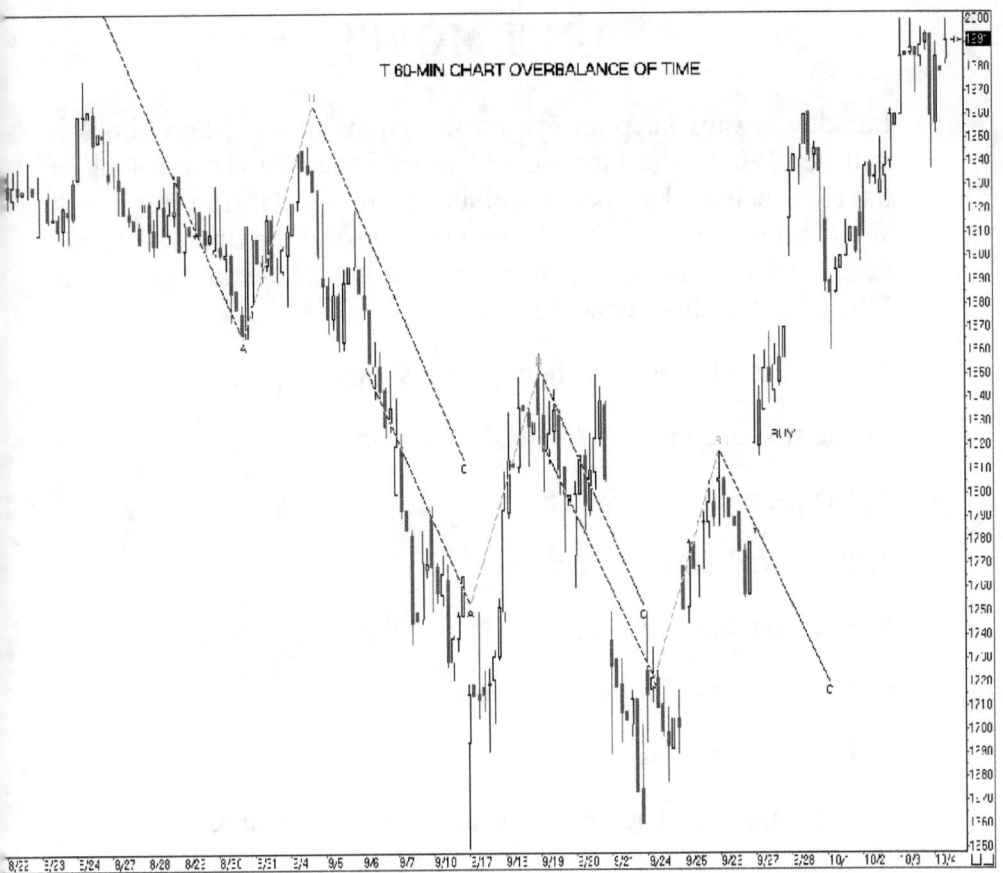

UNIT MOVES

Intraday always keep an eye on the points move. Many times it will be close to the Fibonacci Number Sequence. Take a look at the chart below. This is a 30-minute chart of A.G. Edwards. Look at the number counts. (You'll find that most of the time rallies and declines will only be 1, 3, 5, or 8 units) These are all of the Fibonacci Number Sequence.

1) The first rally from the bottom was 8 units.

2) The first decline was 7 units, just 1 short of 8.

3) The next rally was 3 units.

4) The next decline was 3 units.

5) The next rally was 4 units. One over the 3.

6) There was basically no decline next.

7) The next rally was 5 units.

8) Again there was no decline, showing a strong market.

9) The next rally was 5 units.

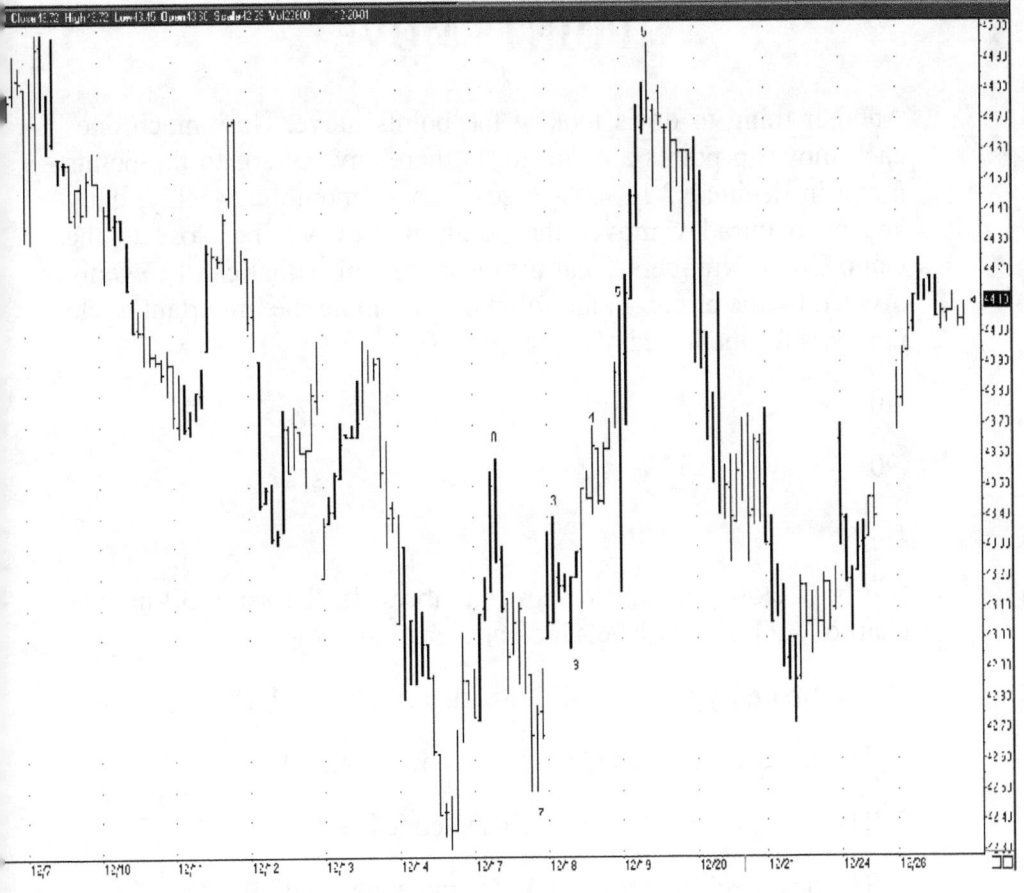

POINTS MOVE

Another thing to do is look at the points move. How much does each move in points amount to. Is there any pattern to the points move in decimals? In most cases in both monthly, weekly, daily and even intraday moves the points moves will be close to the Gann Circle Numbers. That means any number that can be evenly divided by the circle. In the following example the important circle numbers for the intraday move are: .30

.40

.90

1.20

See how close we can to those numbers. In the same 30-minute chart of A.G. Edwards lets look at the points move.

1) The first rally started at 42.31 ended at 43.59 = 1.28

2) The first decline started at 43.59 ended at 42.50 = 1.09

3) The next rally started at 42.50 and ended at 43.40 = .90

4) The next decline started at 43.40 and ended at 42.97 = .43

5) The next rally started at 42.97 and ended at 43.70 = .73

6) The next decline started at 43.70 and ended at 43.44 = .26

7) The next rally started at 43.44 and ended at 44.09 = .65

8) The next decline started at 44.09 and ended at 43.70 = .39

9) The next rally started at 43.70 and ended at 44.95 = 1.25

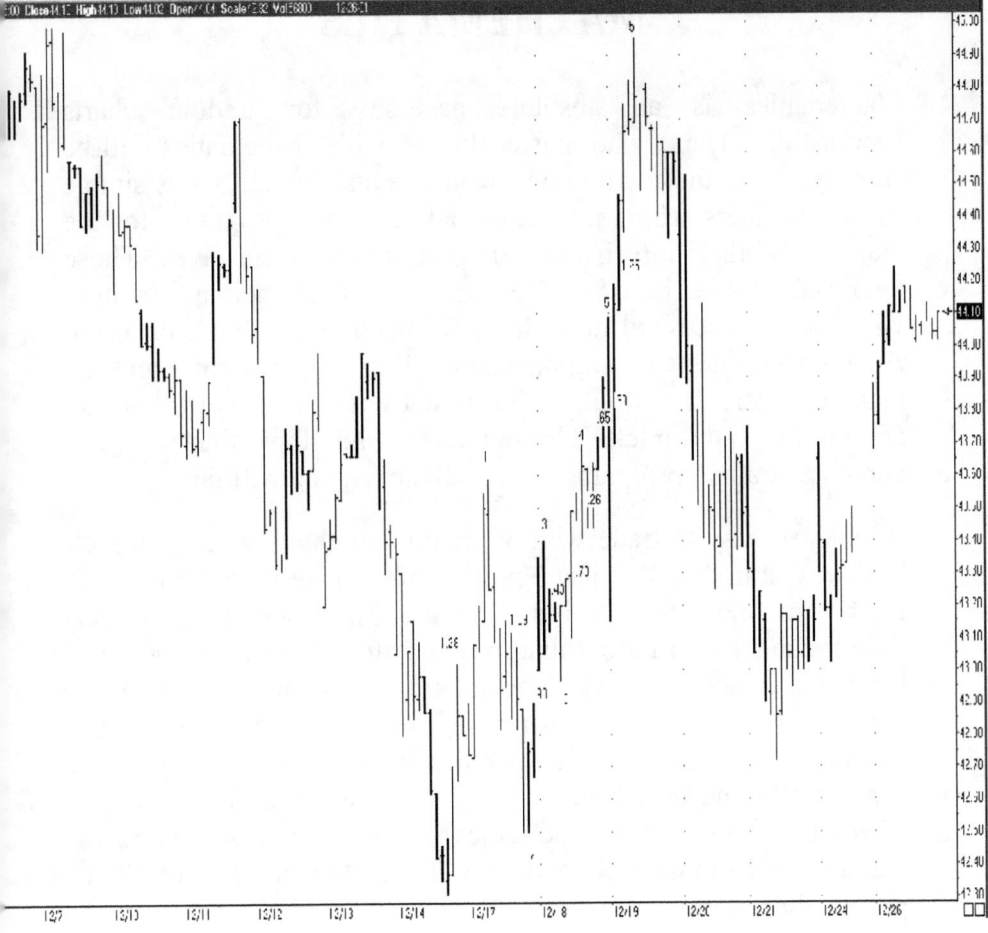

MATHEMATICS

Mathematics is an absolute necessity for trading charts successfully. Those who master this art with mathematics will be successful and those who don't won't be successful. It's as simple as that. Traders who watch financial television programs for the majority of their information are just fooling themselves. Those who make trades based on tips and rumors for their information will not be successful at trading. By reading this book on Gann Analysis you are showing an interest beyond the normal and are making a start. It will take a lot of study and hard work, but you are on the right track. Those traders who think they can use computer-trading programs with oscillators along will fail.

It looks so easy to trade with oscillators on charts when you look back at past trades. You just buy when the stochastic oscillator is at the bottom and sell when it's at the top. Those who try it in real-time trading soon find out that the oscillator will work sometimes, but when it doesn't work. You look all your money. Oscillators tend to work only in non-trending markets. When you get a trending market they won't work because they peg the top of the chart at 100 and they become worthless. Here is an example of a 15-minute chart of AA. Stochastics worked on the first chart. On the second 15-minute chart of AA it didn't work. The oscillator pegged the bottom.

Traders who follow oscillators don't know about cycles. They don't know when the market is reaching major geometric angles from prior highs and lows. They might short the market just when a major cycle low is coming in or the market is resting on a major geometric angle from a market low 5 years ago. These traders end up shorting the market right on a major low and the market explodes and destroys them. If you check around with people who have attempted to day-trade the market with oscillators, you will find that none of them have succeeded. The only traders who make money consistently in the market are the ones that use mathematics. Their trades are based on mathematics and that's what moves the markets.

Oscillators can be used successful in the market, if they are used with the time and price techniques given in this book. In this book we will go over some techniques to successfully use oscillators.

It's a puzzle why most traders don't use mathematics to buy and sell in the markets. It's extremely easy to trade with mathematics after you learn the techniques. It's also much more reliable and consistent. After you get the feel of how to use mathematics you'll never want to just use oscillators again or listen to tips and rumors. You'll find that if someone offers you their view of the market you'll want to shut them out so it does not influence you. You'll also find out that after you have learned the techniques of mathematically trading the markets and you have practiced it for several years that you will develop a sixth sense. Something in your mind will give you an intuition of whether you should buy or sell on points that everything comes together on.

In using mathematics for trading the markets, it's important to know that the market can only move three directions. It can go up, down or sideways. It can't do anything else. This book will give you the mathematical methods to determine which way the market will go. They are based on sound principals, many of which were used by W.D. Gann.

THE CUBE

There are basically three movements of the cube, length, width and height. We use these to figure out market movements. The market can be clocked in time in two different ways. One is calendar days and the other is market days. Intraday you must use market days or rather just units of time. Many traders use both calendar and trading days to check on their accuracy. The market might make a bottom and advance 90 days to the next top. Of course, 90 days is a Gann circle number. That same move would be 126 calendar days if you put in weekends and holidays. How is 90 market days related to 126 calendar days. Both of them are Gann divisions of the circle. 90 market days is exact. 126 is close to the circle number of 120. In all cased there is a direct relationship of market days to calendar days. The relationship is based also upon the golden ratios of .382 and .618. If you take the number 90 and multiple it times 1.382 you will get 124. If you multiple 90 times 1.618 you will get the Gann number of 144. Most of the time the two ways of measurement will coincide with each other. Using the two together will give you a time window of about 3-days for which to make a trade. The ratio of trading days to calendar days is 1.4, which is close to the Gann Square of 144 or 10 times 1.44 or 144, which is a very important number.

The intraday charts using the 60, 30, 15, and 5 minute charts will allow you to get much close in that 3-day window. All the same mathematics that applies to the monthly, weekly and daily charts applies to the intraday charts. There is a simple rule that you can use in all-trading models. The rule for a trading theory to be valid, it must work on all time frames from the year chart all the way down to the minute chart.

Time measurements can be based on several different techniques. One method is to use fixed circle numbers. Those are the numbers that can evenly divide the circle's 360 degrees. These numbers are 9, 18, 27, 3, 45, 72, 90, 120, 180, 270 and 360. You will find that the markets rise and fall on these numbers. The other time measurement technique is to take variable numbers. Those are the numbers based on highs and lows of moves. If a market makes a high at 500 and a low at 200 then the difference is 300. Half of that is 150. This is the mid point when price is likely to go. Often times it will also decline 150 units. This is what squaring time and price means.

RETRACEMENTS – 30-MIN CHART

In the following chart we used a fixed square of 90. The square is actually 1.80 point down and 90 units wide. It fits the action of the market. It is a fixed square based on the fixed circle number. The market actually dropped to the bottom of the square and then retraced almost to the 50 percent market in price.

The vertical or height movement of the market is price. Price calculations can take the same method as price. You can use the natural numbers for this also. Notice below that the times, which is horizontal in nature. The market retraced approximately 50% in time and also began to decline at that time.

A combination of height, width and length of a cube is volume of a cube. The market has to move up and down with enough vibrations to fill the volume of a cube before it can change directions. If you count the swings of a bull market it should equal the swings of a prior bull market. A bear market should also have the same number of swings as a prior bear market.

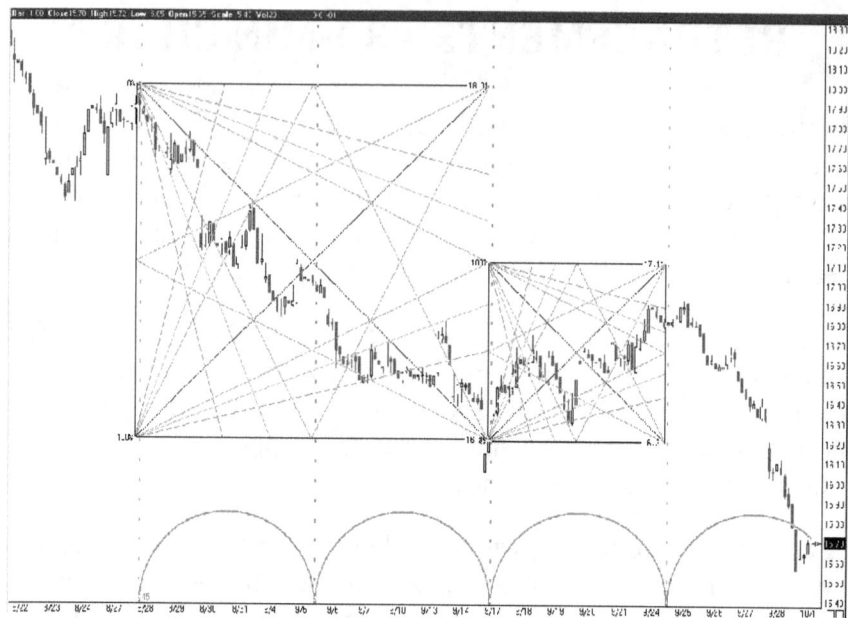

A cube also has six sides. This means that the market will repeat itself every six intervals. That means you should check back every 6 days, 6 weeks, 6 months, 6 years, 60 years and harmonics thereof. Be careful as the market many times has inversions, which means a prior cycle might indicate today should be a high and it is in reality a low. You should also be looking for price patterns so you don't get caught in a price inversion.

THREE BASIC SHAPES

In geometry there are three basic shapes: the square, the circle and the triangle. The square represents both time and price. The horizontal line is time and the vertical line is price. From the square we determine everything both time and price. If we put the circle inside the square and the three sided triangle inside the square that gives us a means of determining time and price points for forecasting markets. Fixed time points are from the circle of 360 degrees. The triangle helps us to divide the circle into 3 different points. These are the 120 degree points. These are some of the most important parts of the circle. The Gann Wheel or as some people call it the Gann Square of Nine is constructed of the square, the circle and the triangle. We use three different basic angles to determine time and price within the markets: 1) The vertical line, 2) The horizontal line, 3) The diagonal line.

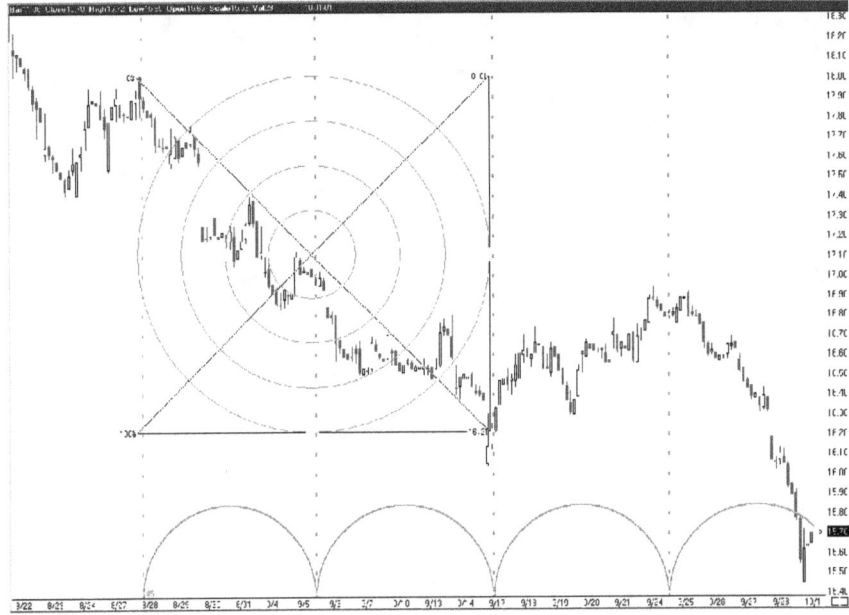

The vertical line is price, the horizontal line is time and the diagonal line is a combination of the two, which is the change of price and time. The triangle can be used to divide the 90 degree points up into 45 degree points. From these three geometric shapes we get all calculations in time and price in the markets. In combination with the angles, we can use the squares of both odd and even numbers to get the cause behind the market movements. These numbers are actually part of the square when they are laid out according to the Gann Square of Nine. In the following example I have place an example of the square, circles and triangles based on the fixed number of 90 from the previous example. Notice has the triangle and the circle points hit the prices so accuracy. This is an additional means to inform you that the square is positioned correctly.

90 SQUARE CHART

The 90 Square Chart is very important to use in trend analysis. See the previous example. To construct the 90 square on your chart first setup the bottom horizontal time units to be 45 or 90 units. Do this with the cycle drawing tool. Once that is done you should next place the Gann Square on the Chart. Find the starting price and add 45, 90 or 180 price units to it to get the top of the square. In the properties of the Gann Square you should check the horizontal and vertical lines you want in the square. Also you need to make sure you check show prices and fan lines in the square.

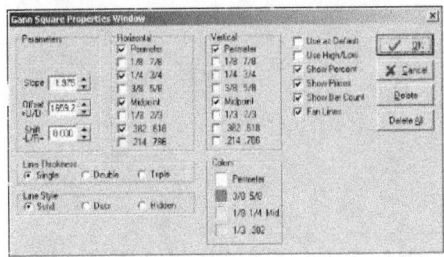

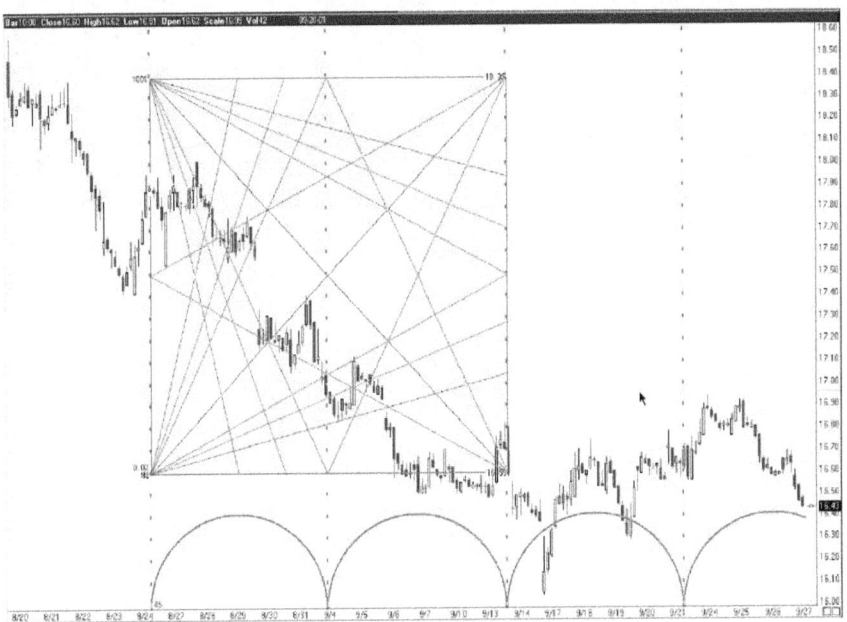

CONSTRUCTING CHARTS PROPERLY

For geometric angles to work properly the charts and the angles must be constructed properly. If they are not constructed properly then one small error can throw off the charts and end up giving you a big loss in the markets. The charts must be constructed with a vertical high, low, close bar. You can use a trade day chart or a calendar day price chart. The trade day chart only has the days traded in it and the calendar day chart has the weekends and the holidays inserted. The calendar day chart is more accurate in time as time continues even during the weekend and holidays. When doing counts on your charts it is very important keep track of important turning points using both trading and calendar days, weeks, months years.

Geometric angles accurate measure time and price movements. There are 360 degrees in the circle and certain numbers in the circle are very important. These numbers will indicate to you when important tops and bottoms are forming. They will also indicate important support and resistance points. You must study and practice with these numbers so you will learn their importance.

Geometric angles are used to measure time and price movements because they are much easier then using addition, subtraction, multiplication or division in the markets. You must use the correct rules for drawing the angles. Angles can correct mistakes in mathematics. For example, if you count across the bottom of your chart 90 units of time and count up 90 units of price and draw a 45 degree angle down from the left high point to the zero point it should intersect at the 0 point with 90 units of price and time.

Have the angles drawn on your chart will always allow you to know the position the market is in at any one time. You will also know when the market will change trend. Geometric angles accurately measure and divide time and price into proportionate parts. If a stock or commodity makes a low on a certain price for example 34, it has three dimensions of time and price. It can move sideways for 34 time units, it can move up for 34 price units and it can move diagonally for 34 time and price units. Accurate measurements can be taken from previous highs, lows and the ranges in between. There is always proportion between previous highs, lows and swings in the market.

Here is an article from Traders World Magazine that explains the 1 X 1 Gann angle in Ensign Software program used in the chart illustrations in this book. The article is by Howard Arrington.

THE 1X1 ANGLE

By Howard Arrington

Every so often some trader engages in a discussion with me regarding the virtues of plotting 45-degree angles on their chart. Invariably their infatuation with this idea is based on a shallow understanding of what a 45-degree line really means, or is supposed to indicate. Their introduction to 45-degree lines is usually from reading something about the works of W. D. Gann and how he plotted 45-degree angles on his charts. Plotting a line on a computer-generated chart physically at a 45-degree angle is worthless. The truth of this statement can be illustrated by

comparing these two charts. See Figure 1 and 2.

The line is plotted at a downward 45-degree angle in both charts, but as can be seen, the line passes through the chart bars in different places. The line, which looks very useful as an indicator of a trend in the left-hand chart suddenly, looks useless in the right-hand chart. So what happened? The vertical spacing of the chart scale changed!Computer generated charts typically use a scale range that covers the highest high and the lowest low of the data set that is being plotted. This scale is mapped to the physical size of the chart window, which might be a couple inches like the examples, or it might be the full size of your monitor display. Not only can the scale range be dynamic, but the bar spacing is also dynamic. The following example uses the same range as the 1st chart, but with a narrower spacing between the bars. The position of the 45-degree line appears quite different now.

The line is plotted at a downward 45-degree angle in both charts, but as can be seen, the line passes through the chart bars in different places. The line, which looks very useful as an indicator of a trend in the left-hand chart suddenly, looks useless in the right-hand chart. So what happened? The vertical spacing of the chart scale changed!

Computer generated charts typically use a scale range that covers the highest high and the lowest low of the data set that is being plotted. This scale is mapped to the physical size of the chart window, which might be a couple inches like the examples, or it might be the full size of your monitor display. Not only can the scale range be dynamic, but the bar spacing is also dynamic. The following example uses the same range as the 1st chart, but with a narrower spacing between the bars. The position of the 45-degree line appears quite different now. See Figure 3.

Since 45-degree lines are so arbitrary in their relationship to the bars, what then was W. D. Gann doing in plotting 45-degree angles on his charts? Gann referred to the 45-degree angles as 1x1 lines (one by one lines). The line was being plotted on his charts with a mathematical slope of one unit of price per one unit of time. Gann would manually construct his charts using graph paper with a square grid. The vertical price grid would be labeled with a price interval such as 2 cents. Thus, the price unit is the grid interval of 2 cents. The bars would be plotted on the horizontal grid, such as a daily bar on every grid interval. Thus, the time unit would be one day.

A graph constructed in this manner would give Gann's 1x1 line the following slope definition: 2 cents per day. A line with this slope could be easily drawn using a 45 degree triangle because of the way the graph paper was laid out. So, a 45 degree line and a 1x1 line with a slope of 2 cents per day would be one and the same thing only when a specific graph paper grid was used.

Computer generated charts with their dynamic scale ranges and dynamic bar spacing must draw 1x1 lines according to a slope definition. The plotted 1x1 line may or may not (usually not) be at a 45-degree angle. When you see a reference to a 45-degree angle, always observe the price grid interval, and the time interval so you know the 1x1 definition for the slope. The slope will be one unit of price for one unit of time. Once the slope is known, the same line can be drawn on a computer generated chart.

In Ensign Windows, the slope of a trend line is shown as one of the parameters for the line. If you want a line to be drawn with a specific slope, you can edit the slope parameter. The slope of the line in the following chart is -250 points per bar. The line will plot in the same position through the bars regardless of changes in the scale range or bar spacing. As changes are made to the chart grid, the angle the line is plotted at will change. The line's slope will remain constant and its relationship to the bars will remain constant. See Figures 4 and 5.

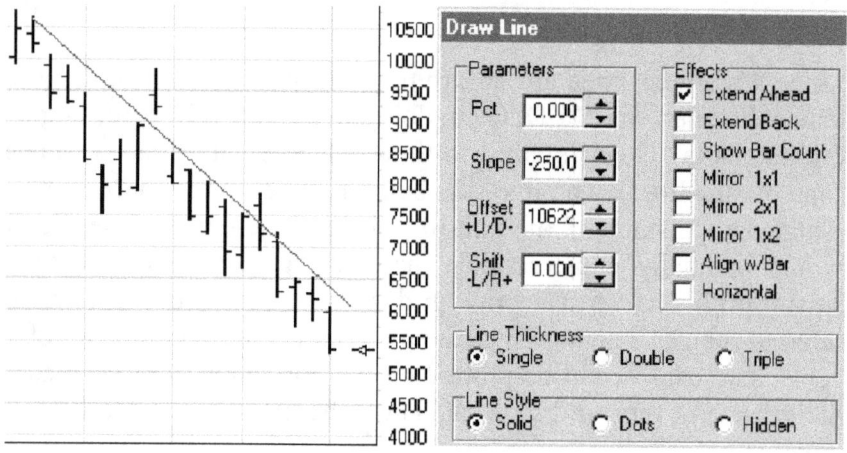

For years, I thought finding a useful slope for the 1x1 Gann line was what Gann analysts meant by the phrase 'squaring time and price.' However, my new understanding is that it is a literal relationship that can be expressed mathematically as:

Price = Time squared or $P = t^2$

For additional information and treatment of this mathematical relationship, please read my 'Time and Price' article in the Spring 2001 issue of the Trader's World magazine. This relationship gives us the needed mathematics for automatically calculating the slope for the 1x1 Gann angle.

To calculate the slope of the 1x1 line, two prices are needed, and a time interval. The first price P1 will be the price on the chart where the 1x1 line (or Gann Fan) is anchored. Usually this is the top or bottom price of a significant trend. The time interval is calculated from P1 by normalizing P1 to fall in the range of 100 to 999. If P1 is below 100, multiply it by 10 as many times as needed until it is in the range of 100 to 999. If P1 is at or above 1000, repeatedly divide it by 10 until it is in the range of 100 to 999. Then the time interval t is found by taking the square root of P1.

Gann's Square of Nine is used to determine the 2nd price P2. P2 is related to P1 by some degree of rotation around the Square of Nine. The commonly used degrees of rotation are 360, 180, 90, and 45 degrees. P2 can be calculated using this formula:

$$P2 = (t + \text{degrees of rotation} / 180) \wedge 2$$

Remember, the time interval t was determined by taking the square root of the normalized price P1. Example: If the trend top or bottom price is $144.00, then the time interval is 12 bars. To find the price that is 180 degrees around the Square of Nine, P2 would be (12 + 180/180) ∧ 2, which equals 13 squared or $169.00.

The slope of the 1x1 line is calculated using this formula:

$$\text{slope} = (P2 - P1) / t$$

Continuing the example, slope = ($169.00 - $144.00) / 12 bars, which equals $2.08 per bar. If the 1x1 line determined in this manner is too steep to be useful on the chart, then it is appropriate to use a smaller degree of rotation around the Square of Nine, such as 90, 45, 22.5, or 11.25 degrees, etc. If the 1x1 line is too flat to be useful on the chart, then it is appropriate to use a higher degree of rotation such as 360 or 720 degrees.

This technology is built into the Gann Fan tool in Ensign Windows. The Gann Fan is placed on the chart by selecting the point for the vertex. The 1x1 line can be located manually by selecting a 2nd point, or let Ensign Windows determine the 1x1 slope automatically using the mathematics developed in this article. The following charts show the Gann Fan with the slope of the 1x1 line determined automatically from the P1 anchor price at the fan's vertex. See Figures 6, 7 and 8.

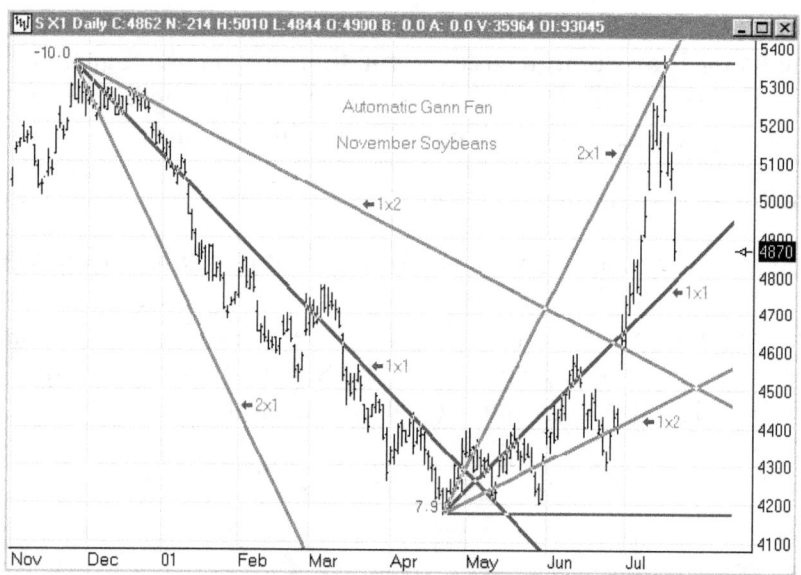

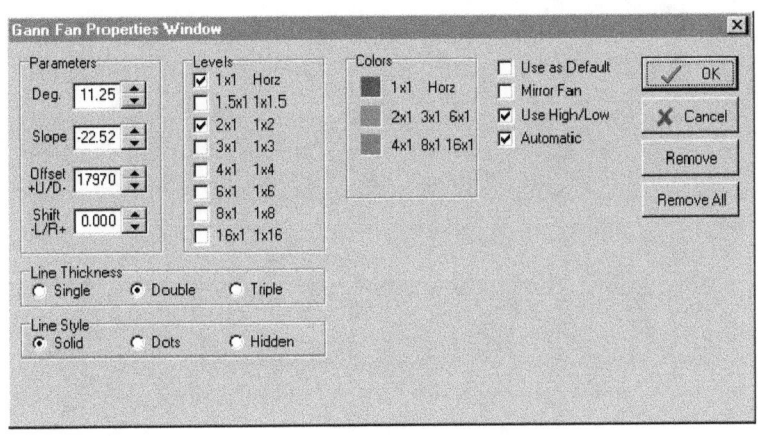

GANN ANGLES

1 X 1 Angle (45-degrees)

The Gann angles are very important to understand. The most important angle is the 1 X 1 angle for the 45-degree angle. You should always draw this angle down from the tops and up from the bottoms. If you draw this angle down from the top and the market gets above it, but later on gaps below it, then it's a sell signal. When this happens you can short the market and put a close stop in to protect your self against reversals. The amount of the stop should be based level of prices and on market volatility which is many times the same. Gann geometric angles will almost always stop a market from advancing or declining the first time prices hit them. Many times the market will go through the angles, if the wave pattern is not complete. If you don't understand wave patterns then you will not be able to fully use Gann geometric angles.

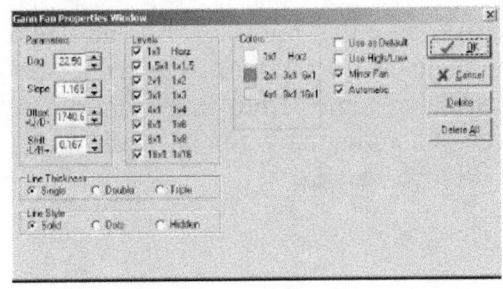

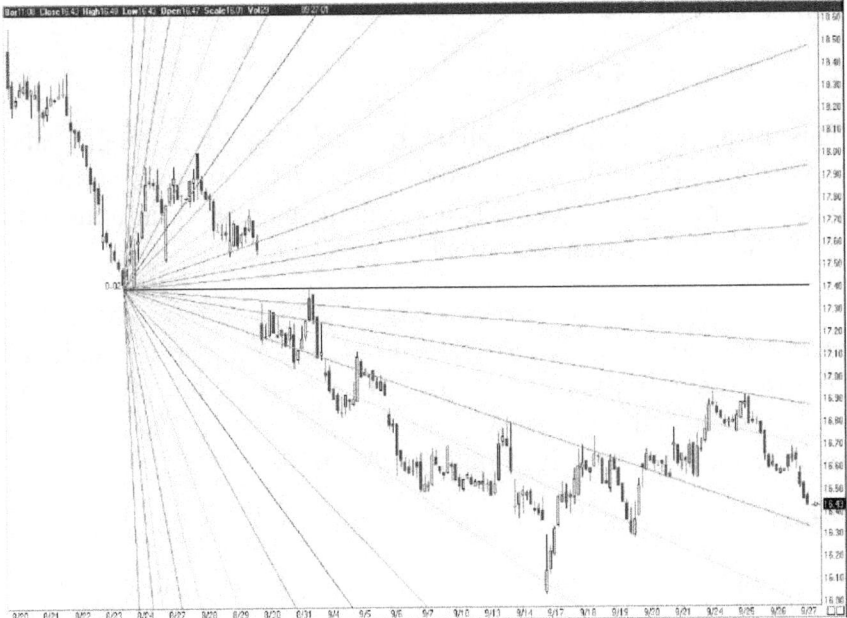

2 X 1 Angle (63 3/4 Degree)

The 2 X 1 angle is the second most important angle. It divides the space between the 45-degree angle and the 90-degree angle. When a market is above this up trending angle it is in a very strong position. If the market breaks this angle, then it will fall to the 45 degree angle.

4 X 1 Angle (75 Degree)

When the market is above this uptrend steep angle, it is in strong

75

position. This is many times the angle that blows off on and when you can make tremendous amounts of money with. The move that starts off from these angles usually comes from important major time cycles that hit the market. When the market breaks below this angle, then it will go to the next lower angle.

8 X 1 Angle (86 1/4 Degree)

When the market is above this angle, it is in a very strong position. It rarely happens on the daily chart but more likely on the weekly or monthly chart. When the market breaks below this angle then it will go the to 4 X 1.

16 x 1 Angle (71 1/4 Degree)

This is a very important angle on the long term weekly and monthly charts after the market has been in an uptrend for an extended period of time. When the market breaks this trend line there should be a change of trend.

When do you draw the angles on the chart? You draw them only after the market has been in a down trend for at least 3 units of time and then market has a rally for three units of time making higher highs and higher lows. The units of time can be 5, 15, 30, 60-minute, daily, weekly, monthly or yearly bars.

Drawing Bear Angles

After the market makes a top using some of the rules for tops, which you will learn in this book, and it breaks the 1 X 1 angle, you start using the next angles down which are the bear angles. The first angle down from the 1 X 1 is the 1 x 2 (26 Y2 degree). When prices drop to this angle the market will bounce off this angle and hold it for a while, however, when the price eventually breaks it, it will go to the next angle down.

4 X 1 Angle (15 Degree)

The next angle down of support is the 4 X 1 (15 degree). When prices hit this angle they will again rally, but eventually when the angle is broken prices will drop to the next angle.

8 X 1 Angle (7 1/2 Degree)

Then the next angle of support is the 8 X 1 (7 Y2 degree). This is very often an important angle of support. After a market has had a long term down trend this angle many times is the angle that turns the market around back to an uptrend. This angle is very important to use with weekly and monthly charts.

1 X 16 Angle (3 3/4 Degree)

The next angle of importance is the 1 X 16 (3 3/4 degree). When this angle is hit there is usually a small bounce as the market is in a weak position.

3 X 1 Angle (18 3/4 Degree)

This angle is very important to use on long-term charts such as weekly and monthly. When you begin to use this angle on the long-term charts you will see it's importance as a timing angle.

When to use Bear Angles

After the market has made a top using the rules of this book and has broken a previous bottom and has declined for 3 units of time, 5, 15, 30, 60 minute bars, days, weeks or months, you can begin drawing the downtrend bear angles.

Start with 1 X 1

Start by drawing the 1 X 1 downtrend angle. When the market is below this angle, it is in a very weak position.

Then Use Other Bear Angles

When the market is below the 1 X 1 down trending angle you can use many of the other bear angles below the 1 X 1.

Under the 2 X 1

The market is in the weakest position when it is under the 2 X 1 angle. The weakest position is when it is below the 4 X 1 angle and the next weakest position is when it is below the 8 X 1 angle.

Gapping Above the 2 X 1 Angle

When the market is in a downtrend and crosses the 2 X 1 angle to the upside especially by gapping it indicates it is in a stronger position and it has a chance to rally. This, of course depends on how long of a downtrend the market has been in.

Moving Above the 1 X 1 Angle

When the market has been in a long trend down and finally crosses the 1 X 1 angle it indicates that the market has changed it's direction. When the market has rallied at least 3 units of time, 5, 15, 30, 60-minute bars, 3 days, weekly or months you can begin drawing up trending bull angles on the chart again. The market is beginning to change into a bull market.

Approaching the 2 X 1 Angle

After the 1 X 1 angle has been crossed, the first down trending angle to draw is the 2 x 1. Crossing this angle puts the market in a stronger position.

Next High Angle is the 4 X 1.

The next angle to draw is the 4 X 1.

Next Angle is the 8 X 1

The next angle to draw is the 8 X 1.

When to Draw Bull Angles

When the market has crossed the 1 X 1 and rallied to the 2 X 1, it will run tin selling and back off. When it gets up through the 4 X 1 and the 8 X 1 finally, it means the market is in a very strong position once again. You should now draw the bull angles up from the bottom.

3 X 1 Angles on Weekly and Monthly Charts

Keep in mind always to watch the 3 X 1 angle on long term charts. When this angle is crossed many times the long term market direction has changed.

Practice with Angles

Practice with all of these geometric angles over and over again. Knowing how to put these angles on your charts will tell you the position of the market at all times. The 1 X 1angles should be put on all previous major highs and lows. The 1 X 1 should be drawn on all zero points. This means if the market either reaches a major low or major high on a certain date a 1 X 1 angle should be drawn on 0 all the way up on the chart. This angle can be calculated mathematically by figuring out where the angle will be coming up from so you don't have to have a chart going down to the point of 0. Also remember for geometric angles to work effectively, you must know the wave position of the market. That is the secret as to when the market will stop on any one particular angle. Sometimes is necessary to draw the relevant angle rather than the 1 X 1. In the below example we used the 1 X 2 and the 2 X 1 angles.

In the following examples we have drawn the relevant 1 X 2 and 2 X 1 angles on all the major tops and bottoms of this 30-minute chart of IBM. See how easy it would be to develop and trading method with this chart. The following is how we set the properties. Notice that we have only checked the 2 X 1 and 1 X 2 angles. Also we have checked the Minor Fan, which allows for down angles and Automatic, which keeps the angles correct according to W.D. Gann.

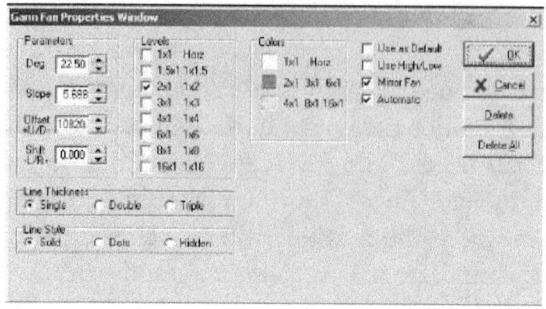

The bottom chart is the first reaction on the above chart enlarged. If you notice the first angle coming up from the lows gives you the approximate top of every reaction. The second angle coming up is the one, which gives you the clear, sell signal when it's finally broken when market prices close under it.

Draw Fixed Number Lines

Another thing that you need to do with a chart is to draw the major circle division horizontal lines on the chart. These again are the numbers that can be divided by the circle. It works of course better on the bigger charts such as the daily, weekly or monthly charts. Intraday charts of 5, 15, 30 and 60 minutes are usually too small of ingredient prices. In the follow examples we have drawn the important circle numbers of 18, 30, 36, 45, 60 and 72. See how good these numbers hit the highs and lows.

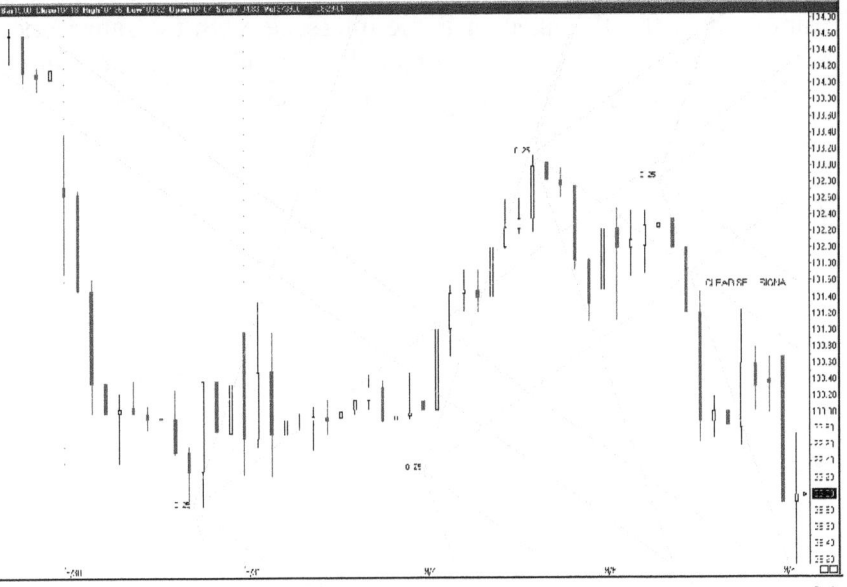

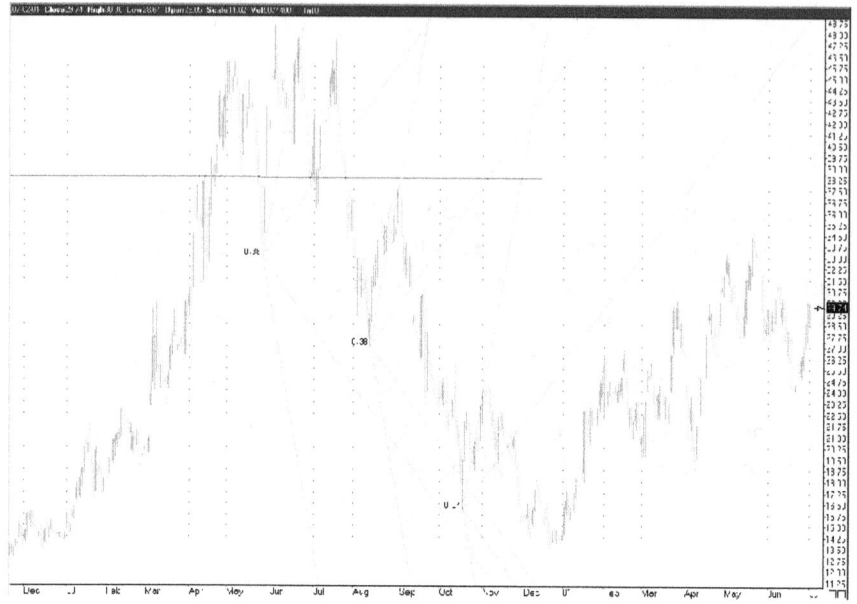

Draw Top and Bottom of Range Lines

You should also draw the horizontal lines for both the top of the range and the bottom of the range. All major and minor angles will square when they intersect with these lines. Notice in the following example how the first steeper angle intersects with the range lines and gives the exact top. Many times the second angle intersecting the horizontal range lines also gives you important timing tops.

THE TIME FACTOR

The most important factor in determining market movements is time. Time tells the trader when the market stops its trend and goes the other direction. If you know the time changes in the markets, then your chances of success will be increased many times.

All time is determined from the circle of 360 degrees:

Divide the circle by 4 parts and you get:

360

270

180

90

You can break these numbers down even further:

45

22.5

11.25

Divide the circle by 3 parts and you get:

360

240

120

You can break these numbers down even further:

60

30

15

7

3.5

3 Times the odd and even numbers and doubling them is very important. Take 3 x 3 (the odd low number) and double them to get the following important numbers:

9

18 38 72 144

288

Take 3 x 4 (the even low number) and double them to get the following important numbers:

12

24

48

96

192

The number 9 is very important as it is the number that ends your count before you start

over, see the following:

1, 2, 3, 4, 5, 6, 7, 8, and 9

add 1 to get the next set

10, 11, 12, 13, 14, 15, 16, 17, 18, and 19

The number 7 is also very important. Many courses start over after the number 7. Also

the following multiples of the number 7 are important.

7

14

21

28

35

42

49 very important

Minor time trend changes will therefore occur every

3, 5, 9, 11.25, 14, 15, 18, 21, 22.5, 24, 28, 30, 35, 36, 42, 45, 48, 49, 54, 60, 72, 90, and 96 days.

Intermediate time trend changes will therefore occur every 120, 144, 180, 240, 270, 288 and 360 days.

Long term time trend changes occur every 3.5, 7, 11.25, 15, 22.5, 30, 45, 60 and 90 years.

BUILT UP FORCES

If a market moves sideways for units of time the accumulated forces of volume will push the market rapidly to catch up with the time. Watch carefully for breakouts out of long sideways ranges. When the markets breakout they will often run up 30 to 49 units of time in one direction.

A daily or monthly chart sideways trend will even give a more powerful breakout. These longer term sideways formations store tremendous power and should be bought on any breakout to the upside.

Here is an example of a 30-minute bar chart of A.G. Edwards. Notice the breakout lead to substantial rally of 30 bars to the upside.

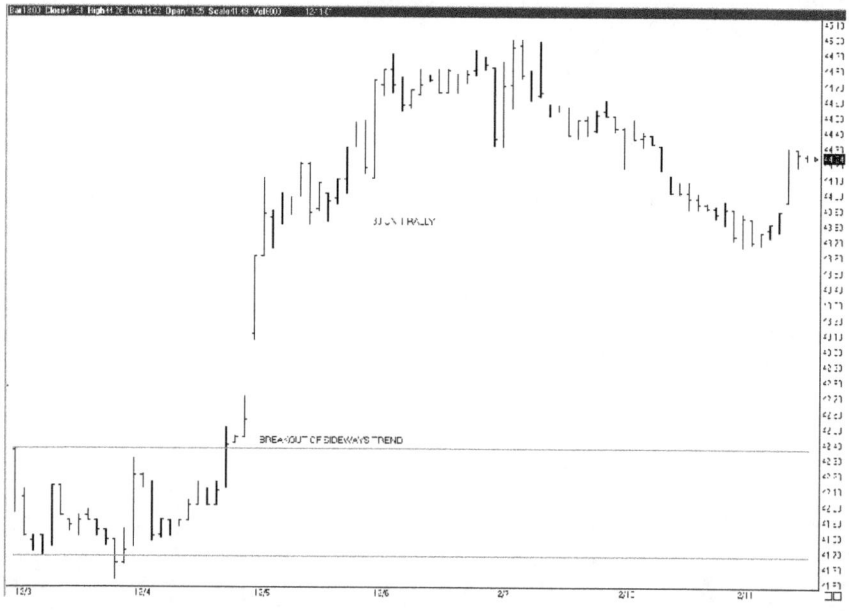

HARMONICS

When you find what long-term trend cycle a stock or commodity is working in you can easily see the harmonics of the move. For example on a 90-year cycle every 9 years will give a good harmonic high or low. On a 60-year cycle every 6 years will give a good harmonic high or low. This is another check to see what time cycle you are really in.

Check back on the harmonic time cycle years to determine what the market might do today. For example if you are following a 90 year cycle, pull the charts every 9 years back to see what the market did in the past on the exact date you are one right now.

The 10-year cycle is the strongest harmonic. It's extremely important to go back every 10 years to determine what the market did during a particular day. You should go back in years:

5

10

20

30

40

50

60 Master Number

70

80

90

100

The 60-year harmonic cycle, which is the master number, is the strongest. 30 years would then be the next strongest cycle, which is half of the master number.

The data to use for this long-term analysis is very difficult to find. Many Gann traders find themselves looking through the microfilm at libraries that carry old issues of the New York Times Newspaper. Many of the traders who have collected this data will not part with it.

Look at the following example of TXN comparing one past harmonic year. The time comparison is 7/16/96 to 10/21/96 comparing that to 7/16/01 to 10/21/01. This is a harmonic cycle of 5 years back.

TXN DAILY CHART YEAR 1996

TXN DAILY CHART OVERLAY

In the following example we have place one chart on top of the other and matched up the exact dates. In the first half of the year the two charts were opposite. The cycle of one was inverted with the cycle of the other. After 11/21/01 both the chart are in perfect harmony. They are following each other's trend almost to the day. Both charts are in sync after that date.

What you will find in looking at the 10 long-term charts is that all of them may go in one direction. If you have this you have a perfect trading situation. If you don't have this then you have to find the past charts it's following best for cycle determination.

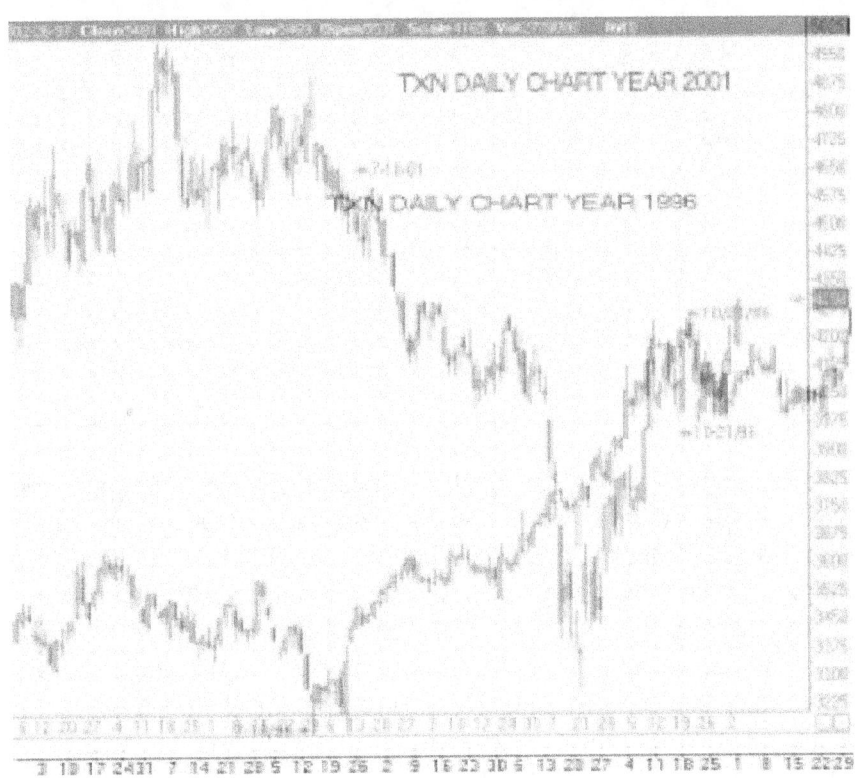

FINDING THE MAIN TREND

Gann used several techniques to find the main trend. The first technique he used was long-term harmonics. That means going back all of the harmonic years and comparing the price trends with today. The harmonic time cycles are taken from the circle of 360 as are all-important cycles.

The most important time yearly cycles are:

90

80

70

60

50

40

30

15

10

5

If possible you should go back on these charts and compare the trends with today. If 10 out of the 10 charts of above are in an uptrend, then there is a high probability that today's trend will be up also. If 5 charts are up and 5 are down, then it's a mixed picture. Many times some of these years will follow the price trend of today almost exactly to the day. Anniversary highs and lows are sometimes made to the day! It's quite amazing sometimes. Gann always said that nothing ever changes. Everything that happened in the past will again happen in the future.

In the previous chart of TXN we compared the year 2001 with the year of 1996. During the swing period of 7/16 to 10/21 the chart are exactly opposites. Chart 2 is an inversion of chart 1.

MONTHLY MOVES

Markets often move on the basis of one year. Therefore it is important to watch divisions of the year. Divide the year into 4 parts. Watch for changes on the end of 3 months, 6 months, 9 months and 12 months. Many changes occur between the 9 and 12-month period. Look at the chart below. It is a daily chart of November Soybeans. The end of every three months is marked with a red line. There is a major change after every red line hit. The changes in price action are substantial. As a trader or even an intraday trader you must be aware of these changes coming in the markets.

MARKET ACTION

As prices get higher on the charts they move faster and faster and have even wider swings. When prices drop to new lows, they will have lower volume and smaller ranges. If you look at Gann's Square of Nine you will notice that the prices between the fixed-cross angles are wider than the ones near the center of the square.

The trend of a market is determined by three different factors.

1) Breaking angles

2) Breaking tops

3) Breaking bottoms

When these are broken important time factors should be nearing their end. When an intraday point is broken like a 5, 15, 30 or 60-minute chart, the market will many times move up to 49 units. When a daily point is broken the market will often move 3 to 10 days. When a weekly market point is broken the market will usually only move 3 weeks. When a monthly point is broken the market will move only 3 months. When a year point is broker the market will move up to 3 years in one direction.

When a market is very slow it may not have enough to get to a time and price point. On the other hand when a market is fast moving it may go through the time and price point because of its inertia.

The market is in its strongest position when its price is equal to the square of its time. When the market tops at 54 and drops 54 units of time, which could be 5, 15, 30 or 60-minute bars, daily, weekly or monthly charts it will square itself. You can expect the market to reverse if it stops at that level and moves sideways for 3 to 4 days and goes the other way. When the market gets above the square price and does so with velocity you can expect a big move in the same direction. If you use the Gann angles discussed previously, they will tell you what position the market is in. Usually the breaking of a 1 X 1 or 1 X 2 angle indicates the market has broken a major angle and will indicate a major change of trend.

When you know the exact life of a futures contract you can also break the cycle up into odd and even numbers. You will find important time changes occur during the intermediate divisions of the contract.

The third, fifth and seventh period on anything very often is a major trend change and the market goes the other way. Watch carefully for 3, 5 or 7 units of time. This is especially true when the market has moved a long way.

Time and space movements can be used in conjunction with time factors to determine changes in trend. For an example of space movement when a contract of corn has been dropping 14 cents on prior reactions and the next reaction drops 20 cents, look for a change of trend. For an example of time movements – when a contract of corn has been dropping 12 days on prior reactions and the next time it drops 23 days, look for a change of trend. These changes also occur during intraday trading with the 5, 15, 30 and 60-minute time bar charts. These changes are very important to watch. They can give you an early warning signal that a change of trend is beginning to happen and action should be taken.

When for example a market goes up 30 cents in corn in 30 days then the market has squared itself. The squaring of time and price will many times indicate a market has changed its trend. Watch this carefully.

Go back and check how long a market normally moves. For example, some markets make a practice of moving at least 5 months. You can break the normal movement of a market into 4 parts to determine when it might end. The fastest part of the move will begin in the 3rd or 4th section.

Geometric angles will tell you what time cycle the market is moving in. When a market breaks an important angle the market will start a new time cycle. It is important to note that the new time cycle may start a different time than the one ending.

Check back on the market you are studying to see what cycles it normally trades in. What cycles it has been trading in will be the same as today. These numbers give you approximations of where the market stops and starts in its time cycles.

The 45-day cycle will usually give you a clear indication of the direction of the market. When prices drop down into a 45-day cycle the prices should then rise. When prices go up into a 45-day cycle the price will then usually turn down after the cycle hits.

Most markets will usually run up or down and stop on 3, 5 or 7 days or weeks. Each market has its own characteristics.

LONG-TERM SUPPORT AND RESISTANCE

In trading the markets, it is very important to know the important force of both support and resistance. Every top or bottom in the market has some relation to some prior top or bottom and it is mathematically based on that prior top or bottom. By using trend lines and time cycles with support and resistance levels, you can do much better in trading and know where to put your stop loss orders.

Take the high price and the low price and divide it by odd and even or 3 or 4. If you want to go down another degree divide it by 6 or 8 or even 12 or 16 levels. When the market approaches these levels of support or resistance and is starting to show a possible change of trend, it is a place to either buy or sell. The halfway points are always the most important. The market will many times hold at these levels for 3, 5 or 7 days, 3, 5 or 7 weeks or 3, 5 or 7 months and give you a chance to buy or sell it. It depends on if the trend is minor, intermediate or major.

When the market moves up to a resistance level or comes down to an important support level its volume and price activity will slow down for several days. The price pattern is usually in a narrowly traded range. Watch the activity closely for a change in trend. It will usually make its move in the direction that it will be going. You should then go with the trend.

You can also divide the highest price the stock or futures ever sold at. Divide it by odd or even numbers to get the support and resistance levels. Again the halfway points are the most important.

If the market ever breaks through it's all time high, the market has no overhead resistance and it many times surges with tremendous strength and volume. Whenever the market breakout out into new highs go with the trend as there is no resistance. In the stock market it is a profitable practice to buy the stocks that are making new highs as these are the strongest stocks in the market.

You can take odd and even multiples of the lowest price the market ever sold at for support and resistance levels. If the markets all time low is 133 then multiply it by 2 to get 266. If that is in the current price range area, then use the number. If it's not in the current price range then multiply 133 by 3 or 4 to get the next price levels.

If that market ever breaks into all time lows it usually is a good idea to short the market and go with the weak trend. The market is in its weakest position when it is making new lows. Everyone that is long the market has a loss and is anxious to get rid of their position when ever the market rallies. Many times the market does not rally when it makes new lows, it just goes lower. Many longs panic and get out of the market and the prices even go lower.

When a market is very fast, it will often penetrate a resistance level temporarily and then bounce back. This often happens at the 50% midpoints of the market. If the market stays above the 50% market, then there is a good chance the market will hold and start to rally when time factors turn up.

Study past action of important support and resistance levels to determine what it will do in the future. The best past action to study is previous same price levels. Also study previous same harmonic time areas such as every 6 years, if the market is following a 60-year cycle. If this is a 45-day cycle low, then you also need to study previous 45-day cycle lows to see how they bottomed.

Previous Futures Contracts High/Lows

It is very important to know when the market has gone through a previous contract high or low. When prior bottoms or tops are crossed, look for a change of trend. When a previous top, which was resistance, is crossed, it then becomes support. When a previous bottom, which was resistance, is penetrated, it then becomes resistance.

Opens and closes are important to determine support and resistance levels. In strong bull markets there are never more than 2 days, weeks, months prices closing lower than the open. The market comes back to close higher than the open and continues its trend.

In bear markets there will never be more than 2 days, weeks, months prices closing higher than the open. The market will usually close lower than the open to continue its trend. Watch the opens and closes especially near important support and resistance areas.

Watch carefully at the beginning of the year in January or in the mid point of the year at July for changes of trend. Watch the first 3, 5, 7 days of the period. If the trend is sideways for those few days and then breaks out, go with the trend. That is the direction of the market. The trend started then will usually last from 3 - 4 months.

Watch the years of extreme high or low prices. These years are very important for support and resistance and determine future movements usually in some important harmonic time measurement. Look carefully at the last number of the year. For example, many times a market will make highs or lows with the same last digit. For example the market might make highs on years that end with 9. See the years 1969, 1979 and 1989. If the market made highs on those years then look for the year 1999 to be a high also. Every market is different so always check back on your long-term historical data.

Watch these time periods carefully. The market is usually just marking time while it squares out some prior top or bottom. When the market breaks out of this range, it usually is a major change of trend.

In all markets you should find the all time high and divide it either by odd 3 or even 2 or 4 to get important support and resistance areas.

You should also multiply the all time low by either odd 3 or even 2 or 4 to get important support and resistance areas.

Support and resistance lines and halfway points can often be used to draw Gann angles. If you have an important high or low you can put your Square of 90 overlay on a high or low and move it up or down to the various support and resistance line. You will be surprised how the Gann angle lines then hit.

Gann said that prior tops and bottoms and their midpoints gave you important resistance and support points. These are to be watched carefully even trading on intraday charts. You certainly would not want to short into a long-term resistance level or buy right into a long-term resistance level on the long-term charts.

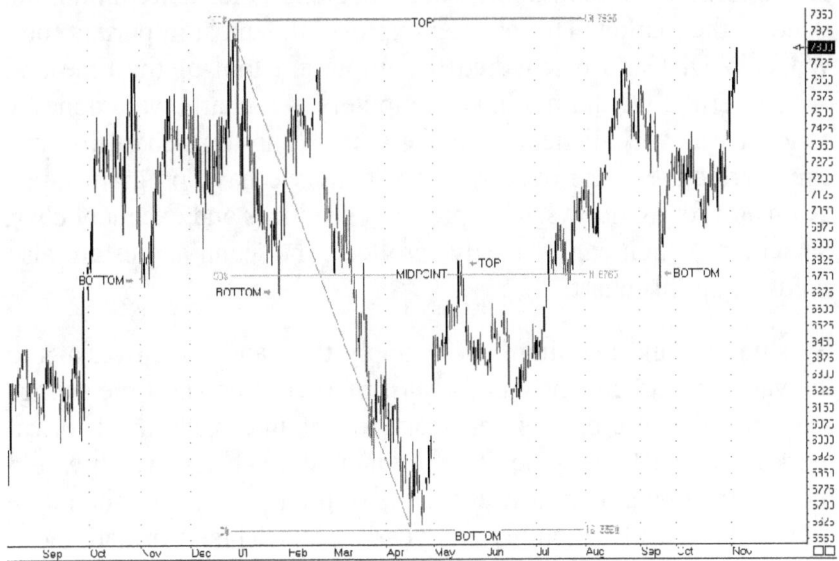

TIME AND PRICE OVERLAYS

In his last years, W. D. Gann said that one of his most important discoveries was the time and price overlay. By using it you could save enormous time in doing your calculations for determining the trend of the market. This chapter explores this most important tool. When W.D. Gann discovered the important tool of the time and price overlay, we did not have computers. All charts were done by hand. It was very difficult to make a nice long-term chart that you could effectively use overlays on. Today we have programs such as Ensign for Windows. This program produces and excellent chart on screen, which can be easily scrolled. The Gann angles are also accurate on this chart.

By studying and learning how to apply time and price overlays to the various markets one can forecast market price and time swings long into the future. It is necessary to obtain long term historical market data such as in the form of Gann style charts, which would include the open, high, low and close of the market. This should be on a daily, weekly, monthly and yearly basis. This information can be obtained from many historical data services. We have found that CSI data to be the most accurate. It is important that the data be linked together correctly. The most effective format of data is the Gann style, which links data together from year to year. This means that December 1992 corn would be linked to December 1993 corn and December 1994 corn would be linked to the December 1993 corn on a continuous basis. Nearby continuous charts link the nearest futures contracts together. This provides a chart similar to the cash markets, but is not as effective in using the overlays. The cash markets and stocks do not need any linking method. They both work very nicely with overlays.

There are two kinds of time and price overlays one can construct to indicate resistance points in the markets. They are the permanent and the variable type. They can be used separately or together to indicate time and price resistance points. The following is a description of each. Permanent time and price overlays give natural resistance points. These resistance points are fixed and based upon key important natural numbers. These overlays help one understand why markets move the way they do. The time and price resistance points formed from these overlays are permanent and do not change. You will learn through trial and error which permanent overlays should be applied to which stock or commodity.

The following is a listing of all time highs and lows for many actively traded commodities on the Chicago Board of Trade. The Gann 1/8 divisions of these all time highs and lows are extremely important and represent strong support and resistance lines.

COMMODITY ALL TIME HIGHS AND LOWS

The following is a listing of some of the all time high and low price for many of the actively traded commodities. The source is the Chicago Board of Trade

Commodity	All Time High	All Time Low
Mar Wheat	645 - 02/26/74	43 - 12/28/32
May Wheat	636 - 02/26/74	43 1/4 - 12/28/32
Jul Wheat	585 - 02/26/74	43 3/8 - 12/28/32
Sep Wheat	582 - 02/26/74	45 1/4 12/29/32
Dec Wheat	582 - 02/26/74	41 1/2 - 11/25/32
Mar Corn	409 - 10/04/74	21 - 02/27/33
May Corn	413 - 10/04/74	22 3/4 - 05/09/1897
Jul Corn	411 - 10/4/74	23 1/4 - 05/29/1897
Sep Corn	388 1/4 - 10/04/74	19 1/2 - 09/08/1896
Dec Corn	400 - 10/04/74	20 3/4 - 12/23/32
Mar Oats	207 - 10/04/74	15 1/4 - 02/27/33
May Oats	208 1/2 - 07/30/74	15 3/4 - 03/02/33
Jul Oats	202 1/2 - 06/14/76	14 7/8 - 06/30/1896

Sep Oats	198 1/2 - 7/30/74	14 1/2 - 09/08/1896
Dec Oats	203 - 07/30/74	13 7/8 - 12/03/32
Jan Beans	961 1/2 - 10/04/74	171 - 12/24/41
Mar Beans	969 - 10/04/74	200 - 06/28/49
May Beans	1076 1/2 - 04/22/77	67 - 07/26/39
Jul Beans	1290 - 06/5/73	75 1/2 - 06/17/40
Aug Beans	1175 - 06/26/73	238 1/2 - 08/07/62
Sep Beans	1010 - 07/25/73	241 1/4 - 08/20/53
Nov Beans	956 - 10/04/74	191 1/4 - 02/06/50
Jan Bean Oil	4787 - 10/04/74	700 - 09/30/68
Mar Bean Oil	4676 - 10/04/74	707 - 10/09/68
May Bean Oil	4588 - 10/04/74	715 - 10/09/68
Jul Bean Oil	4512 - 10/04/74	700 - 07/09/68
Aug Bean Oil	4740 - 07/31/74	711 - 07/09/68
Sep Bean Oil	4490 - 07/30/74	705 - 10/08/68
Oct Bean Oil	5100 - 10/01/74	691 - 10/11/68
Dec Bean Oil	4885 - 10/04/74	695 - 10/09/68
Jan Meal	29000 - 08/14/73	4260 - 01/13/58
Mar Meal	28300 - 08/14/73	4320 - 01/13/58
May Meal	32150 - 05/10/73	4370 - 05/21/57
Jul Meal	45100 - 06/05/73	4335 - 06/25/57
Aug Meal	41350 - 06/05/73	4375 - 06/19/67
Sep Meal	36500 - 06/26/73	4290 - 01/23/58

Dec Meal   29700 - 08/18/73   4280 - 06/19/57

Overlays can now be constructed and used on charts using the Ensign software program. See the following overlay, which as constructed with Ensign.

Permanent time and price overlays are based on divisions of the circle. They can be applied to the measurement of both time and price. The following is a list of the most important resistance levels:

Divisions of the circle by 2, 3, 4, 5, 6, 7, 8, 9, and 12.

360	/ 1	=	360
360	/ 2	=	180
360	/ 3	=	120
360	/ 4	=	90
360	/ 5	=	72
360	/ 6	=	60
360	/ 7	=	51
360	/ 8	=	45
360	/ 9	=	40
360	/ 12	=	30

Overlays can be created based on the above numbers. Some traders have the entire set of overlays made up. They overlay each one on top of prices to find the one that best fits. Some times more than one overlay works. So it maybe necessary to use 2 - 3 overlays to guide you to the price trend.

The following is a listing of the most popular overlays, which are based on the above circle numbers:

Description   Base Number

Square of 12   3

Square of 19   4.75

Square of 27   9

Square of 36   9

Square of 40   10

Square of 45   9

Square of 52   13

Square of 90   9

Square of 180 9

Square of 360 9

Square of 144 12

The basic square is drawn by dividing a square from all corners and sides into equal divisions. The corners are divided by odd number angles 3, 5, 7, 9 etc. This is because time is based on odd numbers. The sides are divided by even numbers of 2, 4, 8, 16, 32, 64 etc. Sides represent price, which is divided by even numbers. In most cases it is not necessary to go all the way out in divisions.

Most permanent time and price overlays are based upon the numbers 1 to 9, but more specifically on the number 9, which is the number that represents the end of the number series upon which all numbers are based upon. In other words beyond the number 9 all ordinary numbers are just a repetition of the first 9. For example, the number 10, as the zero is not a number, it just becomes a repetition of the number 1. The number 11 repeats the number 2, 12 repeats 3, 13 repeats 4 and so on.

Overlays with other base numbers are based on time numbers such as 12 for the 12 months of the year or 52 for 52 weeks of the year. These give you a three-dimensional time view of the market.

Basic Numbers 1   - 9

1 = 10 reason (1+ 0 = 1)

2 = 11 reason (1+ 1 = 2)

3 = 12 reason (1+ 2 = 3)

4 = 13 reason (1+ 3 = 4)

5 = 14 reason (1+ 4 = 5)

6 = 15 reason (1+ 5 = 6)

7 = 16 reason (1+ 6 = 7)

8 = 17 reason (1+ 7 = 8)

9 = 18 reason (1+ 8 = 9)

The fact is the squares that really work well are based on the repeating number of 9. Let's take an example for this repeating number square. Say a commodity bottoms at 42.6. If you add these numbers together (4 + 2 + 6 = 12 and 1 + 2 = 3) if you place the left bottom on that price, the top right will land on 49.80. Now ad this number. (4 + 9 + 8 = 21 and 21 = 3). That's the same number as the bottom.

Variable time and price overlays are developed around major tops and bottoms for a particular commodity or stock. Variable time and price overlays can be used together with permanent time and price overlays for time and price resistance levels and movement for a particular commodity or stock. You should study these overlays carefully and learn how the resistance and support point act on them at different levels.

Squares can be worked up for a specific commodity or stock based upon their contract low.

Besides using lows to set up squares one can also use contract highs. Use the all time high of a particular contract for it's balancing square.

Besides using contract highs and lows, contract ranges can also be used to set up balancing squares.

It is important to combine the natural squares, especially the square of 9 and 13 with the contract high, low and range squares to indicate the time and price resistance points for each stock or commodity. When natural time square points complement the same points given by the variable squares it creates an extra strong points for resistance. In other words if a commodity was working in the permanent square of 144 and the variable square of 43 and they both hit a day the same time, it would be considered a very important turning point. Odd and even squares and halfway points usually give strong resistance points for time and price. The following is a listing of some of these points.

Odd Squares and Halfway Points

Sq of	Is	
9	3	Halfway
		17
25	5	
		37
49	7	
		65
81	9	
		101
121	11	
		145
169	13	
		197
225	15	
		257

289	17

	326

361	19

Even Squares and Halfway Points

Sq of	Is	
4	2	Halfway
		10
16	4	
		26
36	6	
		50
64	8	
		82
100	10	
		122
144	12	
		170
196	14	
		225
256	16	
		289
400	20	

TIME AND PRICE OVERLAYS

In his last years, W. D. Gann said that one of his most important discoveries was the time and price overlay. By using it you could save enormous time in doing your calculations for determining the trend of the market. This chapter explores this most important tool. When W.D. Gann discovered the important tool of the time and price overlay, we did not have computers. All charts were done by hand. It was very difficult to make a nice long-term chart that you could effectively use overlays on. Today we have programs such as Ensign for Windows. This program produces and excellent chart on screen, which can be easily scrolled. The Gann angles are also accurate on this chart.

By studying and learning how to apply time and price overlays to the various markets one can forecast market price and time swings long into the future. It is necessary to obtain long term historical market data such as in the form of Gann style charts, which would include the open, high, low and close of the market. This should be on a daily, weekly, monthly and yearly basis. This information can be obtained from many historical data services. We have found that CSI data to be the most accurate. It is important that the data be linked together correctly. The most effective format of data is the Gann style, which links data together from year to year. This means that December 1992 corn would be linked to December 1993 corn and December 1994 corn would be linked to the December 1993 corn on a continuous basis. Nearby continuous charts link the nearest futures contracts together. This provides a chart similar to the cash markets, but is not as effective in using the overlays. The cash markets and stocks do not need any linking method. They both work very nicely with overlays.

There are two kinds of time and price overlays one can construct to indicate resistance points in the markets. They are the permanent and the variable type. They can be used separately or together to indicate time and price resistance points. The following is a description of each. Permanent time and price overlays give natural resistance points. These resistance points are fixed and based upon key important natural numbers. These overlays help one understand why markets move the way they do. The time and price resistance points formed from these overlays are permanent and do not change. You will learn through trial and error which permanent overlays should be applied to which stock or commodity.

The following is a listing of all time highs and lows for many actively traded commodities on the Chicago Board of Trade. The Gann 1/8 divisions of these all time highs and lows are extremely important and represent strong support and resistance lines.

COMMODITY ALL TIME HIGHS AND LOWS

The following is a listing of some of the all time high and low price for many of the actively traded commodities. The source is the Chicago Board of Trade

Commodity	All Time High	All Time Low
Mar Wheat	645 - 02/26/74	43 - 12/28/32
May Wheat	636 - 02/26/74	43 1/4 - 12/28/32
Jul Wheat	585 - 02/26/74	43 3/8 - 12/28/32
Sep Wheat	582 - 02/26/74	45 1/4 12/29/32
Dec Wheat	582 - 02/26/74	41 1/2 - 11/25/32
Mar Corn	409 - 10/04/74	21 - 02/27/33
May Corn	413 - 10/04/74	22 3/4 - 05/09/1897
Jul Corn	411 - 10/4/74	23 1/4 - 05/29/1897
Sep Corn	388 1/4 - 10/04/74	19 1/2 - 09/08/1896
Dec Corn	400 - 10/04/74	20 3/4 - 12/23/32
Mar Oats	207 - 10/04/74	15 1/4 - 02/27/33
May Oats	208 1/2 - 07/30/74	15 3/4 - 03/02/33

Jul Oats	202 1/2 - 06/14/76	14 7/8 - 06/30/1896
Sep Oats	198 1/2 - 7/30/74	14 1/2 - 09/08/1896
Dec Oats	203 - 07/30/74	13 7/8 - 12/03/32
Jan Beans	961 1/2 - 10/04/74	171 - 12/24/41
Mar Beans	969 - 10/04/74	200 - 06/28/49
May Beans	1076 1/2 - 04/22/77	67 - 07/26/39
Jul Beans	1290 - 06/5/73	75 1/2 - 06/17/40
Aug Beans	1175 - 06/26/73	238 1/2 - 08/07/62
Sep Beans	1010 - 07/25/73	241 1/4 - 08/20/53
Nov Beans	956 - 10/04/74	191 1/4 - 02/06/50
Jan Bean Oil	4787 - 10/04/74	700 - 09/30/68
Mar Bean Oil	4676 - 10/04/74	707 - 10/09/68
May Bean Oil	4588 - 10/04/74	715 - 10/09/68
Jul Bean Oil	4512 - 10/04/74	700 - 07/09/68
Aug Bean Oil	4740 - 07/31/74	711 - 07/09/68
Sep Bean Oil	4490 - 07/30/74	705 - 10/08/68
Oct Bean Oil	5100 - 10/01/74	691 - 10/11/68
Dec Bean Oil	4885 - 10/04/74	695 - 10/09/68
Jan Meal	29000 - 08/14/73	4260 - 01/13/58
Mar Meal	28300 - 08/14/73	4320 - 01/13/58
May Meal	32150 - 05/10/73	4370 - 05/21/57
Jul Meal	45100 - 06/05/73	4335 - 06/25/57
Aug Meal	41350 - 06/05/73	4375 - 06/19/67

Sep Meal   36500 - 06/26/73   4290 - 01/23/58

Dec Meal   29700 - 08/18/73   4280 - 06/19/57

Overlays can now be constructed and used on charts using the Ensign software program. See the following overlay, which as constructed with Ensign.

Permanent time and price overlays are based on divisions of the circle. They can be applied to the measurement of both time and price. The following is a list of the most important resistance levels:

Divisions of the circle by 2, 3, 4, 5, 6, 7, 8, 9, and 12.

360 / 1 = 360

360 / 2 = 180

360 / 3 = 120

360 / 4 = 90

360 / 5 = 72

360 / 6 = 60

360 / 7 = 51

360 / 8 = 45

360 / 9 = 40

360 / 12 = 30

Overlays can be created based on the above numbers. Some traders have the entire set of overlays made up. They overlay each one on top of prices to find the one that best fits. Some times more than one overlay works. So it maybe necessary to use 2 - 3 overlays to guide you to the price trend.

The following is a listing of the most popular overlays, which are based on the above circle numbers:

Description	Base Number
Square of 12	3
Square of 19	4.75
Square of 27	9
Square of 36	9
Square of 40	10
Square of 45	9
Square of 52	13
Square of 90	9
Square of 180	9
Square of 360	9

CHARTS

The important future months should be watched for key signals. A good set of charts should include the key months of future contracts of the year in commodity future contracts. For example, in most commodities the 12th and 6th positions of the cycle of the year are important. These are December and June. The next important commodities are the 3rd and 9th positions, which are March and October.

The time increments are important. When trading correctly, you should have daily, weekly, monthly and yearly charts. If possible the chart should go back to the beginning of the contract. If that is not possible then you should at least have the all time high or low on the chart. Weekly charts are the most useful for long range trading. If you are trading intraday you should have 5, 15, 30 and 60-minute charts.

It is very important to have the necessary update space on your chart so you can do long range forecasting. On a daily chart the update space should go out 1 year. On the weekly chart the update space should go out for 2 years and on a monthly chart the update space should go out for 5 - 10 years. The Ensign for Windows charts do allow the necessary update and projection area on the right side of the chart.

Man has learned to measure time with calendar periods. The larger the calendar period, the more important it is. Different time periods should be used to get the trend of the market. You should always know what direction each of the time periods is in. It will make you a much more effective trader. Watch closely for a change of trend in each time frame and trade accordingly. In order of importance the following are calendar periods most used:

Important Time Frames

Yearly - for long term

Monthly - for long term

Weekly - for intermediate and long term

Daily - for short term

60 minute - for short term

30 minute - for short term

15 minute - for short term

5 minute - for short term

HOW TO USE THE OVERLAY GANN SQUARE

It is recommend that you get monthly, weekly and daily charts of the markets you want to trade. These are the charts that W.D. Gann used. For effective intraday trading get the 60-minute, 30-minute, 15-minute and 5-minute charts. All these charts must have adequate update space to the right of the chart for updating and forecasting future trends. By using all of these charts your perspective of where the market is will greatly improve.

The long-term charts should be back for at least 30 years. They should have update space for at least five years. They are the best charts to use for effective long-term time counts. They also give you excellent price support and resistance levels. These charts often change every 3 months. The weekly chart is probably the best long-term chart to trade from by the average trader. The chart should have 5 to 10 years of data on it and at least 2 years of update space. You will find that these charts often will change trend every 3 - 12 weeks. This is an excellent chart to use verify that the monthly charts are changing trend.

The daily charts are used by most traders, from computer programs to chart services. These charts should be at least 3 years in length and have update space of 1 year. Most losses occur because of these charts because people do not know how to trade them. These are the charts that you will use to enter and exit the market after both the monthly and weekly charts have changed trends. The scale on these charts is very important. Gann tried to use a 1 to 1 scale in most cases. You will have to experiment with the scale so it is right. Commodities like corn, wheat, oats, and the S&P might be on a scale of 1 to 1. You'll have to experiment with this scale to get it right. The intraday chart is the most difficult chart to trade with. More people lose money using this chart than any of the others. For the beginner 60 or 30 minute charts are recommended. Used properly they can help your entry into the market. After the monthly, weekly, daily charts have all changed trends, use these charts to enter or exit the market with precision. For these charts, you'll have to have real time or delayed data from an on on-line service such as Signal.

To use the Gann Square Overlays they should be overlaid over price charts in the following fashion

1. The bottom/left corner of the square should be placed below the exact bottom on the date of the bottom. This will show the important support angles pointing up.

2. The top/left corner of the overlay should be placed above the exact highs on the date of the high. This will show the important resistance angles running down from the top.

3. The square overlay can also be placed on 1/2 of the highest high. It can also be placed on an important circle number or a table number.

4. It can also be placed on 1/2 of the range. The angles will indicate support or resistance where they hit price.

5. The bottom/left corner can also be placed on the 0 low under and major high or low.

6. It you use an MACD oscillator the square can also be placed on a momentum high or low which not necessary the price high or low.

7. The top/left high can also be placed over the anniversary date or 1/2, 1/4 or 1/3 of the anniversary of a high 1, 2, 3, 4, 5 etc. years out.

TIME AND PRICE CHARTS

Let's go into the explanation and use of Gann's master time and price charts. Perhaps the most interesting of these charts are the odd and even square charts. The odd chart is commonly known as the square of 9 and the even chart is known as the square of 4. The square of 9 has the number 1 at the center and spirals clockwise around the square. The even chart has four numbers in the center 1, 2, 3, and 4. It spirals counter clockwise around the square. Each of the chart's parameter is divided into dates and degrees of the year that go counter clockwise. Each circle of the square of nine ends with an number that squares out (9, 25, 49, 81, 121, 169, 225, 289 etc.). Each circle of the square of 4 ends with an even number that squares out (4, 16, 36, 64, 100, 144, 176, 256 etc.). Which of the two charts to use depends on the total days in the contract from beginning to end. You must look up to see when the first day of trade was and look up the last day of trade. If there is an even number of days in the contract use the square of 4. If there are an odd number of days in the contract use the square of 9. There are many different ways to use these charts. One useful way is to set the beginning day of trade at 1 in the center of the square. As the contract trades out in time, you can see resistance at the completion of each circle in the square. You can often tell which chart (odd or even) a commodity is following by where it ends in time. Use calendar days for this timing. The Excel template available to you has the ability to be configured into either entirely dates, numbers or a combination of both. That means you can set the center to the beginning data and price of the contract and easily see all of the resistance dates and prices all the way out. The center can also be set to a major low or high date of price to see all of the resistance dates and prices.

The Square of 9

This is a very important chart because nine is our number's system key. Nine is the basis of everything. When we count up to the number 9 we must start the count over to get to 10 (9 +1). Look at the square of nine chart in this chapter. The first major opposition is at 9 x 9 = 81. This completes the first square of 9. The second square of 9 ends at 162, the third square of 9 ends at 243, the fourth square of nine ends at 324 and the fifth square ends at 361 (19 x 19). Watch for these major oppositions when the market is trading in both time and price resistance. Important resistance points are on the fixed cross which is on the horizontal and vertical lines intersecting the center. These are the numbers 6, 19, 40, 69, 106, 151, 204, 265, 334 etc. going to the right. Going to the left are the numbers 2, 11, 28, 53, 86, 127, 176, 233, 298. Vertically the numbers are 4, 15, 34, 61, 96, 129, 190, 249 and 316 and down vertically the numbers are 8, 23, 46, 77, 116, 163, 218, 281 and 352. The cardinal cross numbers are also very important resistance points. These numbers are 3, 13, 31, 57, 91, 133, 183, 241 307, 7, 21, 43, 73, 111, 157, 211, 273, 343, 5, 17, 37, 65, 101, 145, 197, 267, 325, 9, 25, 49, 81, 121, 169, 225, 289 and 361. The square of 9 chart is an excellent tool to help you forecast the markets. This tool can help you to significantly increase your accuracy in forecasting changes of trend in the market. Look at the square of 9 chart and find the number 496. Moving up on the chart the market finds price support as follows:

Degrees	Support/Resistance
45	485
90	474
120	463
180	452

Moving down on the chart the market finds support and resistance in the following areas in the degrees of 45, 90, 120, and 180.

Degrees	Support/Resistance
45	507
90	518
120	529
180	541

The market will also find support and resistance with dates at those same areas of price. For example on March 21 you will find the following resistance and support on these dates.

Degrees	Support/Resistance
45	May 6
90	June 21
120	Aug 8
180	Sep 23

Look on the chart at the numbers running down from the center to bottom left date of November 7. They are squares of odd numbers and represent support and resistance. The numbers are 1, 9, 25, 49, 81, 121, 169, 225, 361, 441, 529, 625, 729, 841, 961, 1089. The numbers running up from the center to May 6 are even squares of even numbers. The numbers are 4, 16, 36, 64, 100, 144, 196, 256, 324, 400, 484, 576, 676, 784, 900, 1024. The numbers 90 degrees between these squares of both even and odd numbers are midway points of support and resistance in both time and price. The major trend in both time and price is the year and minor trends are the divisions of the year, which the square of 9 chart gives. Major trends will reverse most of the time with the minor trends as follows using the following trends:

Trend	Rates as to Importance
45 day	2
90 day	1
120 day	6
135 day	4
180 day	3
225 day	8

270 day	5
315 day	7
144 day	9
216 day	10

Major Year Changes of Trend

The major yearly long-term trends usually terminate on their anniversary dates. They are confirmed by the minor trend directions. For example after a major trend has topped, the minor trend may have a 45 day bottom to high and a 90 day bottom to high trend reversing the market down. See the following rules concerning vibrations of trend direction.

Rules of Vibrations of Trend Direction

When the trend ends at the high it is assumed the market will turn down. When the trend ends on the low it is assumed the market will turn up. Follow the next 4 rules concerning this. Study the historical market of each commodity or stock to determine which particular trend from 45 - 315 day has turned its trend in the past.

1) When the vibrations of trend start moving from low to high the trend is turning down.

2) When the vibrations of trend start moving from high to lower high the trend is turning down.

3) When the vibrations of trend start moving from high to low the trend is turning up.

4) When the vibrations of trend start moving from low to higher low the trend is turning up.

Using the Square of 9 for Forecasting

The square of 9 has become very popular for forecasting time and price. Many expensive Gann wheels have been sold in the last few years. The Gann square of 9 in the Excel template program is an electronic version of one of those expensive wheels. In fact it is much better, because it is precisely accurate. It's based on formulas. For ease of use you may want to create a simple plastic overlay which fits over your computer screen. The advantage of this overlay is that it can be rotated over the square of 9. This is something that the Excel spreadsheet program can't do yet. If you want to, of course, you can figure the points out on the screen without the overlay using the drawing lines in the program. The square of 9 is important, because it is based on the number nine. The number nine is the basis of our entire number system. The square of 9 is actually known as the Pythagorean Cube. It starts with a small number in the center and then it spirals outward in ever increasing numbers. The first square ends with the number 9, the second square ends with the number 25. All of these numbers can be exactly squared (3 x 3 = 9, 5 x 5 = 25 and so on). The outside of the square of 9 has both the 360 degrees of the circle and calendar dates of the year on it. This is programmed into the Excel template. The dates include the four quarters of the year starting with the Spring Equinox (March 21st) on the right. The Summer Solstice (June 21st) at the top. The Fall Equinox (September 23rd) at the left and the Winter Solstice (December 21st) at the bottom. These dates run counter clockwise.

The overlay that you can make to overlay on your computer screen can divide the square of 9 into 45-degree sections, 120-degree sections and 144 degree sections. Also on the overlay can be indicated important timing dates such as Fibonacci numbers of 1, 2, 3, 5, 8, 13, 21, 34 55 and so on and lunar 30 day cycles. Also weekly numbers of 5 can be placed around the circle of 5, 10, 15, etc. Also good to put on the overlay is the important death zone of Gann, which are the 42 to 55 calendar days.

Here is How to Use the Overlay

When the market makes an important low or high on a particular date, you should place the overlay on top of the square of 9 on your computer screen. Rotate the overlay so that the 0 point is on that date. Now look on the overlay over 45 days to get the important date of a possible change of trend. The 45-degree line is actually minor resistance. The next 45-degree line over is the next resistance, which is 2 x 45 or 90 degrees. This represents major resistance. The market almost always goes through to the 90-degree point in time. The 0 line on the overlay should be placed on the price of the market low. 45 and 90 degrees over in price represent resistance in price. When the time arrives for the possible change in trend, watch where the price is. If it's at one of the angle lines, it's probably major resistance and a major change of trend will usually occur. Sometimes when the market is very strong in one direction it can continue its trend through to the next resistance levels in both time and price. It will go to the 120, 144, 216, 270, 315 and 360 levels in both time and price. Watch all the points carefully for changes in trend. Also watch the Cardinal Square and Fixed Cross points for resistance in price. Also watch the area of square numbers at the end of each circle for resistance points. Using the square of 9 is an art rather than a science.

TABLE CHARTS

This chapter on table charts has been developed from long experience, cultivation and studious research designed to unravel, at least to some extent, the mysteries of the subject of table charts on which many students of Gann have floundered.

All that admit it the theory of application of table charts for time and price forecasting has been the one side of technical analysis that has been least explored or investigated.

This chapter is designed for the serious-minded student of the commodity and stock market. Presented herein will be the often misunderstood and mysterious table charts that most traders have so much trouble understanding. The ideas on how to use these table charts will remain ideas unless one spends many hours studying each one and proving to his own satisfaction that they work.

All the table charts in this chapter are produced with the Microsoft Excel spread sheet program. The template for this program is available free with this course. This is an excellent piece of software that can save you many hours in constructing these variations of table charts rather than doing them by hand.

Time and price forecasting are the essential ingredients for success in trading the markets. One who can predict time and price movements of the markets can reap enormous financial rewards. Proper interpretation of the table charts should help one anticipate many of the fundamentals that one needs to know long before the general public knows them. Table charts give a mathematical viewpoint of how a market should move with respect to both time and price. With the knowledge table charts gives you, can easily spot the important support and resistance points.

By studying and learning how to apply table charts to the various markets one can forecast market price and time swings long into the future. It is necessary to obtain historical market information such as the first trade day of a commodity or stock, major high and low prices with dates of each. This information can be found from commodity year books, historical data, chart services and from company records.

The more you study commodity or stock price movements, the better you will understand the markets. Working with table charts will help you understand the interplay of the underlying economic forces of supply and demand in the market. This chapter will attempt to help you develop an understanding of price and time movements and provide you with fertile seeds, which, if properly nurtured, should yield success in the field of stock and commodity speculation.

With these few words as a preface, I will endeavor to make the theory and application of table charts so clear that I hope anyone of ordinary education may be able to follow and experiment with certain rules, which will be treated in the following chapters.

Basic Numbers

The table charts presented in this chapter are mathematical sequences of numbers presented in various forms of design to aid the technician in the forecasting both time and price movements in the stock and commodity markets. The charts are based upon the numbers 1 to 9, but more specifically on the number 9 which has to be regarded as the end of the series of numbers, upon which all of our materialistic calculations are built upon. Beyond the number 9 all ordinary numbers are just a repetition of the first 9. For example, the number 10, as the zero is not a number just becomes a repetition of the number 1 The number 11 repeats the number 2, 12 repeats 3, 13 repeats 4 and so one. The following illustration shows why all numbers are just a repetition of the numbers 1 through 9.

Basic Numbers 1 - 9

$1 = 10$ reason $(1 + 0 = 1)$

$2 = 11$ reason $(1 + 1 = 2)$

$3 = 12$ reason $(1 + 2 = 3)$

$4 = 13$ reason $(1 + 3 = 4)$

5 = 14 reason (1 + 4 = 5)

6 = 15 reason (1 + 5 = 6)

7 = 16 reason (1 + 6 = 7)

8 = 17 reason (1 + 7 = 8)

9 = 18 reason (1 + 8 = 9)

The above are sequences of numbers that add up to the indicated based number. Look them over and use the following pages as a reference to those numbers.

Kinds of Table Charts

There are two kinds of table charts one can construct to represent support and resistance points for both time and price in the markets. They are the permanent and the variable number table.

The Fixed Chart

The fixed chart gives you natural resistance points. These natural resistance points are fixed and based upon key important numbers. These tables help one understand why markets move the way they do. The time and price resistance points formed from these fixed charts are permanent and do not change. You will learn through trial and error which table charts should be applied to which stock or commodity. Every stock and commodity has its own square of a number that it works in and that number will never change. The following is a listing of the most commonly used fixed tables.

Square Table Charts

Square of 3 Square of 4 Square of 6 Square of 9 Square of 12 Square of 19 Square of 20 Square of 24 Square of 27 Square of 36 Square of 52 Square of 90

The Variable Chart

Variable table charts are developed around key individual market data beginnings, and major price tops and bottoms for a particular commodity or stock. Variable table charts can be used together with fixed table charts for time and price resistance levels and movements for a particular commodity or stock. Variable table charts can be used together with fixed table charts for time and price resistance levels and movement for a particular commodity or stock. You should study these charts carefully and learn how the resistance points are formed and how to apply them.

The Square Table Chart

The square table chart is the most commonly used forecasting table of all the types available. It has a basic square or rectangle construction. The charts start out in the lower left corner going up in number progression to the top of the square. It then restarts back down at the bottom in row two and starts up again and so on. The following is a description of several of the more popular squares.

The Square of 3 Chart

The square of three table chart 3 up and 3 over. It is the most basic of table charts and represents the importance of the number 5 as the mid point or halfway point of our basic 1 to 9 number system. The number 5 is surrounded on all sides by 4 numbers, the numbers 2, 4, 6, and 8. This table chart is the most basic of all and is the basis of all numbers.

The Square of 6 Chart

The square of 6 chart 6 up and 6 over ending at 36. This first square of 36 is very important for time and price measurement. Six represents one quarter of the hours in the day. Six months is one half of the year. Six is a division of the circle 6 x 60 = 360 degrees.

The Square of 9 Chart

The square of 9 chart which is very important in measuring time and price moves. As we stated earlier in the course the number 9 in our mathematical system is very important. You cannot count beyond 9 without starting over with the number 0. In the square 9 x 9 which equals 81 which completes the first square of 9. The second square of 9 is completed at 162, the third square of 9 is completed at 243 and the fourth square of 9 ends at 324. Completing five squares gives us the important number of 360.

The Square of 12 Chart

The square of 12 chart which is a very important table chart. It is important because of its relationship to the 12 months of the year. It consists of a chart which is 12 up and 12 over which makes the first square of 144 and the fourth square at 576 - all key mathematical resistance numbers. The squares all end on the important 9 numbers. There is (1 + 4 + 4 = 9), (2 + 8 + 8 = 18) and so on. The number 9 is the finality on which all our number calculations are built. This important square can be used to measure both time and price movements. That is, the number of time or price points up or down in units days, weeks, months our years. You can make as many squares as you want to cover any price or time movement. Now lets list and analyze the important areas of resistance in the first square.

1) The Major Center is where the strongest resistance is met. These are the four number in the center of the square - 66, 67, 68 and 69. A stock or commodity going up or down should meet strong resistance here.

2) The Diagonal Resistance Numbers are the second strongest resistance points. One diagonal these are the numbers 1, 14, 27, 40, 53, 66, 79, 92, 105, 118, 131 and 144. On the other diagonal are the numbers 12, 23, 34, 45, 56, 67, 78, 89, 100, 111, 122, and 133.

3) The Diagonal resistance Numbers of Quarter Squares are the third strongest resistance points. These are the numbers 7, 20, 33, 46, 59, 72, 6, 17, 28, 39, 50, 61 and 73, 86, 99, 112, 125, 138, 139, 128, 117, 106, 95 and 84.

4) The Top and Bottom Numbers are next in importance and many times represent important tops and bottoms and halfway points in respect to time and price.

5) The Halfway Point Numbers are next in importance and represent minor tops and bottoms or halfway points in regard to the time and price.

6) The Four Sections of a Square are important for determining resistance of both time and price movement. Divide the square into 4 sections and you get the number 36. Add 0 and you have the number of degrees in the circle. Divide the 36 into 4 minor square and you will get the important number of 9. Divide the number 9 again into four sections and you will get the most important minor division of time and space of 2.25. Now, lets go back to the original 4 sections of the square. Moving over one section on the square of 36 you will reach the square of its own place. Next, when you move over two sections to the number 72, it reaches its halfway point. Three sections over to the number 108 it reaches its third resistance point which in many cases is a very difficult point to penetrate. The fourth resistance point is the hardest of all to penetrate which ends with the key number of 144. If it gets through the fourth section it will then be in the second square of 12, which is 145 to 288. If it maintains this price level with falling back into the first square it will then attempt to go through each section of the second square. Price or time movement will continue to move into each consecutive square trying to penetrate each section of the squares until it finally fails. Most bull or bear campaigns usually fail in the fourth square of 12. In every consecutive square price and time movement volatility increases proportionally. Which is why many times a market ends its campaign with a price blow off

The Square of 19 Chart

The square of 19 chart which is a very important table which is 19 up and 19 over. This square is often called the square of the circle because it proves the circle. The square of 19 x 19 ends at 361 which is just one over the 360 degrees in the circle. At the major center is the number 181, which is one over the half the circle 180 degrees. This illustration shows that when we reach the number 181 we are crossing the center and on the other side of the 360 degree circle. It is important to know that many price movements end with the square of 19.

The Square of 20 Chart

The number 20 which represents the number of trading days in the normal month, and the 18th division of the circle is quite important for measuring both time and price. The first method of counting by man was probably with his hand, which consists of 5 fingers. Finally he probably incorporated his toes, which eventually developed into a system of 4 x 5 = 20. It was then finally possible with a combination of finder counting and memory to reach even larger numbers. Many of the civilizations of the world have used a 20-finger number system. This is the chart Gann used for the New York Stock Exchange. He called it his NYSE Permanent Chart.

The Square of 27 Chart

The square of 27 chart 27 up and 27 over which ends at 729 is close to 720 or 2 times the circle. The number also adds up to the important number 9 the end of your basic number series. Dividing the square of 12 months gives 60.75 years or 1/6 the circle. Dividing each quarterly square then gives 15.19 years and the halfway point is 7.59 years close to the 7 1/2-year cycle.

The Square of 36 Chart

The square of 36 chart 36 up and 36 over which ends at 1296 is important for measuring all time and price movements and resistance points. It adds up to the important number 9 and adding a zero gives the important 360 degrees in a circle. This is a very important square for determining tops and bottoms of the market. The top of the square numbers tend to be highs and the low and mid point numbers are usually lows in the market.

The Square of 52 Chart

The square of 52 chart, which is 52 up and 52 across is a very important square representing the 52 weeks in a year. The square of 52 is 2704, which is 7 years and 5 months very close to the important 7 1/2 year cycle or 90 months.

The Square of 90 Chart

The square of 90 chart which is 90 up and 90 across which ends at 8100 is an important square. The number 90 is one quarter of the circle and adds up to the important number 9. Dividing the 8100 by 365 calendar days gives you 22.19 years to work out the vibration of each square of 90. Dividing this by 4 gives you 5.54 years or 287 weeks, which ends the second square of 12 and divided by 3 gives 7.40 years, which basically is the 7 1/2 year cycle.

Variable Low Squares

Squares can be worked up for specific stocks and commodities based on their contract low. For example on December 28, 1932 March wheat had a low at 43 cents per bushel. The square or balancing of the price is 43 days, 43 weeks, 43 months. The square of 43 (43 up and 43 across) can be worked up for March wheat to use for time and resistance points. For September Wheat the low was made on December 29, 1932 at 45 1/4 cents per bushel. Therefore for this contract one must use the square of 45 to determine its resistance points.

Setting up Contract high Squares

Besides using lows to set up squares one can also use contract highs. Use the all-time high of a particular contract for its balancing square. For example, March Wheat had a high of $6.45 on February 26, 1974. Therefore use the square of 81 (6.45 / 8 = .80626) as its balancing square for this top.

Setting Up Contract Range Squares

Besides using contract highs and lows, contract ranges can also be used to set up balancing squares. March Wheat had an all-time high of 6.45 and an all-time low of .43. The difference between the two is 6.02. Therefore a balancing square of .70 (5.59 / 8 = .6988) per bushel can be set up to indicate resistance points.

Combining Squares for Resistance Points

It is important to combine the natural squares, especially the square of 9 and 12 with the contract high, low and range squares to indicate time and price resistance points for each stock or commodity. When natural time square points complement the same points given by the variable squares it creates an extra strong point for resistance.

Low/ High Number Squares /Natural Time Squares

It is possible to use contract low prices to determine intra cycle resistance points within a time period. For example March Wheat had a low on December 28, 1932 at 43 cents per bushel. A square of 12 with an intra-cycle of 43 can be set up to determine the monthly future cycle points. Since the low occurred on the 12th month in 1932, label the first row as 1932 and circle the number 12. Therefore every 12 thereafter that occurs in the chart will be an important cycle month. It is also possible to use contract high prices to determine intra cycle resistance points within a time period. For example March Wheat had a high of 645 on 2/26/74. Divide this number by 8 to get it down to a smaller number under 100 to make a square with. This gives the number 80.625 or round to the number 81.

FORECASTING TIME

One trader once told me that you can't trade a market unless you know where it is going. W.D. Gann was able to forecast time cycles with amazing accuracy. This chapter tells you how he did most of it. W.D. Gann believed that the future is but a repetition of the past. There are no new things under the sun. By studying the past one can forecast future cycles of the market.

The 120-Year Major Cycle

This is a very important cycle which is 6 times the 20-year cycle, 4 times the 30 year cycle and 2 times the important 60-year cycle.

The 100-Year Major Cycle

This is one of the largest cycles, which you need to watch closely for comparison to the current time period. Watch for price trends that are similar in their direction with current direction.

The 90-Year Major Cycle

This is a very important cycle, which is 3 times the 30-year cycle and 1 1/2 times the important 60-year cycle.

The 80-Year Major Cycle

This is an important cycle, which repeats over and over again in the trading history of the markets.

The 60-Year Master Cycle

This the master cycle that repeats over and over again. You should go back and find past 60-year cycles and compare them to the current cycle. To be very accurate in forecasting time you must know this cycle.

The 49/50 -Year Major Cycle

You should also find the 49 - 50 year cycles in the market. This is a very important cycle. There are seven 7-year cycles in the 49 - 50 year cycle. Watch each 7-year cycle, many times they act the same as prior cycles. For example, the last 7-year cycle in the 49-year cycle is usually down. This knowledge is very important to have.

The 40-Year Major Cycle

The 40-year cycle is most important as it is 1/2 of the 80 year cycle. Watch to see how it closely.

The 30-Year Major Cycle

Watch the 30-year cycle, which is 1/2 of the 60-year master cycle. Each of these 30-year cycles inside of the big 60-year cycles is important.

The 20-Year Major Cycle

This cycle is important, as there are 3 of these in each 60-year cycle. Watch for similar action to determine the trend of this cycle.

The 15-year Major Cycle

This cycle is also important, as it is 1/2 of the 30-year cycle. Watch it closely in conjunction with the 30-year cycle.

The 10-Year Major Cycle

This is a very important cycle as their are 6 of these in the 60-year cycle, 5 of these in the 50 year cycle, 3 of these in the 30 year cycle and 2 of these in the 20 year cycle.

THE 8-Year Major Cycle

This is a very important cycle that often shows up which are 1 year above the 7-year cycle.

The 7-Year Major Cycle

This cycle is also important to watch as there are 7 of these in the 49-year cycle and 14 of these in the 98-year cycle.

The 5-Year Major Cycle

This is a very important cycle to watch, as it is part of every other cycle above. This is the smallest cycle that we look at for comparison purposes.

The 2 /12 - 3 1/2 Year Major Cycle

This cycle is most important as most counter trends react against the main trend with one of these small cycles.

HARMOMICS OF THESE CYCLES

All of these cycles have harmonic years. To get these harmonics just divide the cycle into 10. For example the important 60-year cycle divided by 10 is 6. Therefore every 6 years there will be a harmonic of the major cycle. The 90 and 60-year cycles are the major ones and are very important. It is impossible in most cases to get data going back 60 - 90 years. You have to scan the NY Times for even sometimes cash data to interpolate. The harmonic years give you an idea of what the major cycle is even if you don't have the data. For the 60-year cycle if you go back for example every 6 years for 20-30 years you will have a good idea of what the major 60-year cycle was. This is especially true if every 6 years back the market did exactly the same thing.

The 1 Year and Under Cycle

The cycles under one year are all based on the circle. The cycles inside of the year are the 45, 90, 120, 135, 144, 216, 240, 244, and 270. The 45-day cycle can be broken down even further into 22 1/2, 11 1/4 day cycles. The 120-day cycle can be broken down into 60, 30, 15 and 7 1/2-day cycles. The 144-day cycle can be broken down into 72, 36, 18, and 9 day cycles. It is important to understand that all cycles must fit within each other. The smallest cycle of 11 1/4 is a part of even the 100-year cycle. The cycles in this paragraph make up all the important cycles in the world. Everything is based on these cycles. If you find an important cycle that is not one of these, then it must be a Fibonacci ratio of one of these cycles.

How to Use the Cycles

The most important thing you can do is to watch how the cycles are working. Compare the current cycles with those of the past. Go back to each of the cycle years and compare them to the current ones. You should print out all past harmonic cycle years on translucent paper and overlay them on top of each other. When most of the harmonic cycles are in the same direction then the probability of that direction in the market today is pretty sure. Sometimes when only half of all the cycles are in one direction, you must wait for all cycles to turn in that same direction. 10 or 5 to get harmonics of the big cycles can divide all of the major cycles. Watch those 10 and 5 divisions of prior cycles to determine how the market might move in each future division. Many times each division will have the same exact movement as prior divisions. Watch the major 90 and 60 year cycles as these represent the dominant cycles of the market. If both of these change in one direction, it is almost a sure thing that the market will move in that direction.

Using Daily Charts for forecasting

Daily price movements give the first change of trend in the markets. Watch for the 10-week time period. Also watch for the 7 1/2, 11 1/4, 15, 22.5, 30, 45, 60, 72, 90, 100 day cycles. This works the same as using the major cycles. For example if 10 weeks ago the market started to move up then watch the current time period. If it starts to move up exactly 10 weeks from its last low then it is important.

SHIFTS IN CYCLES

There are sometimes shifts in the major cycles several days from anniversary high or low days. This is caused by progression of time. That means that time has gotten out of sink or has shifted several days. You can find that shift and make allowances for it by looking at the pattern of today and comparing it the pattern of a past cycle. You should use transparent chart paper and overlay them on top of each other and slide the paper to the right or left to allow for that shift of time. There are many cases the anniversary dates of past harmonic cycle years hit the exact date!

Beginnings of time periods (changing of trends)

Watch the first and third week of the beginnings of these important times of the year. Usually a range of days will set up with a high and a low. When prices break out one-way or another the other side of the range becomes resistance or support. In order of importance these are the periods to watch for:

January 21 - Watch the first 5 days March 21- Watch the first 5 days June 21- Watch the first 5 days September 21- Watch the first 5 days

Yearly - Watch the first and third week of January

Semi-Annual - Watch the first and third week of July

Quarterly - Watch the first and third of week of April and October.

You should also divide the year into divisions and watch the first 5 days of each division for a change of trend.

Divide the year into 2 to get 6 months

Divide the year into 4 to get 3 months

Divide the year into 3 to get 4 months

Divide the year into 8 to get 1/2 months

Divide the year into 16 to get 22 1/2 days

Divide the year into 32 to get 11 1/4 days

Comparisons of Years Ending with Same Digit

Go back over the years and overlay all years that end in the same digit. For example for the current year of 1995, you should compare 1985, 1975, 1965, 1955 etc. This can be done easily with Ensign for Windows. The program is windows based and allows windows of the different years to be overlaid vertically on top of each other.

REOCURRING CYCLES

The market normally makes the same amount of moves from its peaks and troughs. You should go back and look at all past cycles carefully. Watch the following combinations to determine the probable cycle length. Write all prior counts down and keep tract of them for future reference. List all of the following in the market:

High to Low, Low to High Top to Top Bottom to Bottom

Those moves can be in both calendar days and market days. To calculate the differences you can use the Excel spread sheet for the calendar days and the master plastic overlays for market days. The two projections will create a time windows for you to trade on.

The following Fibonacci ratios work very nicely. These are the ratios that we have programmed into the Excel spreadsheet See Exhibit 13.4. This is a picture of the Excel spread sheet module for wave forecasting based on those ratios. By inputting three dates in this spread sheet you can get the top-to-top or bottom-to-bottom time calculations. By inputting 2 dates in the spreadsheet you can get bottom to top and top to bottom calculations of timing points.

.382 .500 .618 1.00 1.382 1.500 1.618 2.000 2.382 2.500 2.618

ELLIOTT WAVE THEORY

Gann used pattern and wave analysis also to analyze the markets. In this book we will explain how to use the Elliott Wave Theory, which is now more refined than the wave analysis used by Gann. R.N. Elliott developed his hypothesis in the 1920's. Mr. Elliott discovered there is no disorder in the markets, but conversely this is a natural order in the markets that is clearly illustrated by definite wave patterns, which continually repeat themselves. These wave patterns constantly replicate themselves again and again in the markets. The wave patterns are also fractal in nature, which means that you can subdivide these waves into smaller and smaller waves and they was have the same pattern, just a different degree.

In the 1970's the Elliott Wave Principal was extremely popular because of books published by Prechter and Frost. The most famous book they published was "The Elliott Wave Principle...key to stock market profits" in 1978. Robert Prechter was extremely popular and was frequently interviewed by the news media during the time. He predicted the bull market of the time and even the crash of 1987.

The secret of the Elliott Wave Theory is to learn how to correctly detect these wave patterns that tend to occur over and over again in the markets. These wave patterns can be divided into basically two kinds, the trending wave and the non-trending wave. Some people call them impulse waves and corrective waves. The markets tend to trend only 20% of the time and they go into corrections 80% of the time.

The impulse wave has five price movements. Three of them are in the direction of the market and two of them are in the opposite direction of the market.

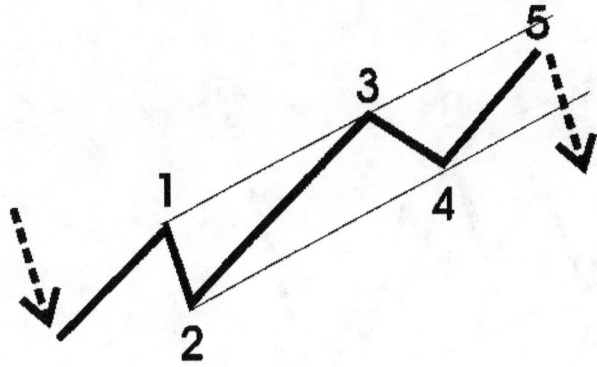

These five waves can also be broken down into smaller waves. Each impulse wave has five waves and each correction has 3

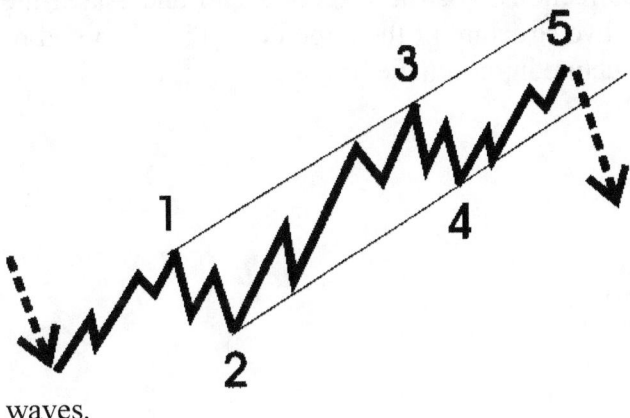

waves.

The corrective waves can also be broken down into a smaller degree. Waves A and C are in the direction of the reaction. This would illustrate the reaction in a bullish trend.

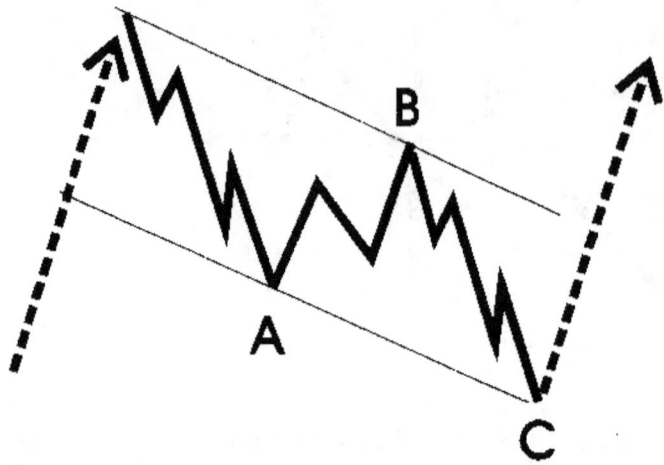

It should be very easy now to distinguish between the trends of the market and the corrections. Also it's important to understand the concept that the wave structure of the large degree is composed of the same wave structure in the smaller degree.

USING GANN RATIOS

There are actually two types of ratios that can be used with waves. They are actually the Fibonacci or Gann ratios. You should check the market you are trading to determine which of the two types of ratios the market is best working with. The following is a listing of the differences in the ratios. Gann ratios are determined by basically dividing the full numbers into halves and thirds as far down as you need to. Here are the ratios used: Divide the number by 2 or 4 or down as far as you need to. By doing this we get the following compared to the Fibonacci Ratios used by most Elliott Wave Traders.

Basic Ratio Differences

Gann .25 - .33 - .50 - .66 - .75 – 1.00 – 1.25 – 1.33 etc. Fibonacci .382 - .618 – 1.00 – 1.382 – 1.50 – 1.618 etc.

As you can see the Gann ratios are very similar to the Fibonacci ratios used by Elliott Wave traders.

FORECASTING PRICE

Price forecasting is one of the most difficult Gann techniques. In this chapter we will go into the techniques that are available. Many of the techniques are different, but in the end they come out to the same price projection. These techniques should be used in combination with the time forecasting techniques. Time must in the end square out with price. In many respects time and price are one and the same thing. Using our Excel template you will find that you can change the format of the squares in a sheet from numbers to time and the same sheet can be used for time forecasting. This includes every sheet in the Excel template that we have programmed for you.

Table Charts

One of the easiest ways of forecasting price is to the table chart. We have all the basic number formats programmed into the Excel template. These table charts work with the internal time structure of the market. This is the vibration rate of the market. This vibration rate is usually based upon the all time low or high of the contract. It may also be based on the beginning or opening price of the contract or stock. It's a matter of trial and error to find the right vibration rate. In many cases the vibration number is based on a key circle number. You can set the number 1 on the table chart to a major high or low and watch the top and bottom numbers on the square. These numbers are quite often the highs and lows of the swings of the market when the table is set correctly. Table charts are programmed so you change the 1 number and every number in the entire table chart changes. Each square has it's own formula except for square 1. Square 2 is based on the formula of square 1 plus 1. Square 3 has a formula of square 2 plus 1 and so on. In the table charts, never change any number but the base number of 1 otherwise; you will ruin the entire table chart. Always keep a backup of your Excel spread sheet so if one of the other squares gets changed by accident, you can replace the entire template with your backup.

Square of 9

The square of nine has become a very popular chart. It can be used in many different ways to forecast price.

Beginning Price or Contract Low

The first way this chart can be used is the set the center number 1 at either the beginning price of the contract or at the contact low. Use the square of 9 on contracts that have an odd number of total contract days. Use the square of 4 for contracts that have an even number of contract days. So if wheat had a low at 43, you would change the number 1 to 43. Every time the square of 9 completes a circle there is resistance at that level. Price meets the square of its own starting price at the end of each circle. When the price exceeds that resistance, it then becomes support. The further the price gets out on the square the wider is the distance between the different resistance and support levels and the wider range of the fluctuations.

Natural Numbers

The second way to use this chart is to leave the center number as 1 and use the numbers at the end of each circle as natural resistance numbers. The other numbers of importance are the numbers at the Fixed Cross (those are the numbers that are vertical and horizontal from the center) and the Cardinal Square (those are the numbers that are X from the center). When price hits the natural resistance numbers there is opposition to advance.

Gann Wheel

The third way to use this chart is to use the 360 degrees and dates around the outside and a plastic overlay divided into the angles of 90, 120, 144, 180, 214, 240 and 270 degrees. When the price of a contract or stock makes a low, you move the plastic overlay 0 point to that price and line it up with the price found inside the wheel. Now continue counter clockwise using the overlay till you get to the 90-degree line. The 90-degree line intersects with the next level of price inside the square. This is resistance. If price gets through this resistance it will go to the next level. The prior resistance then becomes support. Watch for a change of trend at every angle line. Sometimes price will be at an adjacent angle or an opposition angle. Watch the rallies and declines into these angles. If rallies stop exactly on 90-degree lines and go back down, the main trend is down. If declines stop exactly on 90-degree lines and go back up the main trend is up. The secret is the wheel tells you that all counter trends against the main trend will end up on a key angle line. Resumptions of the main trend do not usually end on an exact angle line. They usually go through it. However, when you do notice that the main thrust of a trend does land on a key angle line, then the trend is reversing.

If you keep the 0 point of the overlay on March 21 and look at the prices the angles of the plastic overlay hit, you will find that sometimes the dates on the outside of the wheel hits the same price that an angle is on at the same time. This is called time aspecting price. This is natural time and price resistance. You always check this particular use of the wheel, as it happens too many times to be coincidence. These are very strong points of support and resistance.

Using the Master Overlays

The master overlays should be used to forecast price based on market days. You should create the following overlays on clear plastic in the scale of your charts 45, 52, 72, 90, 120, 144, 216, 240, 270, and 360. They should be used in two different ways. One is to place them on highs and low. This is using it the variable way. From every top or bottom the market will move 45, 52, 72, 90, 120, 144, 216, 240, 270 and 360 points. You can take multiples of the squares also for price projecting. For example the market may move three squares of 144 from a price point. So if for example May Soybeans bottomed at 460 you would place the overlay left bottom on that point and project up 3 squares of 144. (460 + 144 + 144 + 144 = 892)

The squares can also be used the fixed way in that on every major bottom you could place the square at 0 point and project upward for price projections. For example with the previous example of Soybeans at 460 the fixed price resistance points would be at (144, 288, 432, 576, 720, 864, 1008 et c.) remember the more price clusters you have at one point the more important the price point is. You should also check back on all prior tops and bottoms for other indications of support and resistance.

The market will usually work in one of the natural squares of 45, 52, 90, 120, 144, 216, 240, 270 and 360. You must experiment to see which square it is working it. On daily charts in most cases it will be either the square of 90 or 144. In some cases it will work in the square of 120 or 52. You will also find that some of the square work betters with the weekly and monthly charts better than the daily charts. It is just a big process of experimentation and trial and error until you find the right square or combination thereof. Also the market will also work in the square which is usually based on the all time low of the market. For example in May Soybeans the market works in the square of 67, which is the all, time low of that contract. You must make up a master plastic square of 67 for use with that contract. Use this in combination with the fixed square that you use.

Remember the more price clusters you have at one point the more important that point is. Use all the techniques presented in this course to arrive at those clusters. Use both market and calendar days. You will be surprised at the results.

USING CIRCLE NUMBERS FROM BEGINNING NUMBERS

The important circle number can also be used to forecast from important tops and bottoms. These can be put into the time sheet also. Remember the more clusters of timing point out in the future the more important is the projected pivot point. Using the circle numbers of:

45 72 90 120

144

216

240

270

360

Harmonics of Beginning Numbers

The time sheet can also be set to forecast harmonics of the beginning number. For a low of 43 days set the numbers to 43, 86, 129. 172 and so on. This would give you a turning point at every interval of 43.

Square of 9 and 4 for Time Projection

We have also programmed into the Excel template the square of 9 and the square of 4 charts. These charts are an electronic marvel! They are 10 times better than any other Gann wheel, because you can change the center number to a beginning number or date for time and price projection. For time that number should be set a beginning date of a contract or of a minor, intermediate or major bottom.

Using the Center with Beginning Numbers

The square of 4 should be used with a contact with an even number of days and the square of 9 should be used with a contract with an odd number of days. Experiment of with both squares to see which one is hitting the numbers better. For time set the center number to the beginning date of the contract. You will find resistance to advance at the end of each circle and at the Cardinal and Fixed Cross points.

Using Squares with 1 at the Center

The squares can also be used effectively in their natural state with 1 at the center. This gives you the natural numbers from which to find time resistance points. If you locate the prior market tops and bottoms in the square you will find that many of them are on natural Cardinal or Fixed Cross points. These are dates around the outside of the square. If you find the dates hit the same time as the price in the square this is a very significant. This means that the contract is locked in with natural time and resistance points. You will have to use the plastic overlay to match the date on the outside with the inner square numbers. You will have to draw this on a plastic overlay sheet in the scale of your computer screen or print the square out on paper and use it over that.

The overlay divides the square of 9 or 4 up into proportions. Place the 0 point of the overlay on the date a market starts to move. Then watch for a turn in the market over 45, 90, 120, 144, 180, 216, 240, or 270 degrees using the plastic overlay. When you move the overlay to the projected date check to see if the price of the commodity it intersecting the line going through the center to the other side. It is important if the price of the commodity is at an some important angle to the date that it is on. For example, 90, 180, or 120 degrees over. This is called price aspecting. When the market starts to run up in price and intersects at numbers on the 45, 90, 120 degree lines then there will probable be a change of trend. In the opposite fashion if the price starts to decline into the 45, 90, 120 degree points and aspects with key prices then the market will then again have a change of trend.

MMM DAILY CHART T&P SQUARING

Gann said that all tops and bottoms will square themselves out in the future sometime. For example in this case MMM made a low 78.5 at 3-14-00. This means that in the future the stock will square itself out in 78.5 hours, days, weeks, months and years into the future from that point and every harmonic thereof. Look at the below chart and you will see that when it touches on of these Gann lines there usually is a sharp reaction. Usually if it drops under one of these line the market will continue down until it hits the next Gann angle line. Ensign allows you to draw perfect Gann angles. Very few programs on the market are accurate like Ensign. Here are the angles that he program allows you to draw:

1x1,   horz

1.5 x 1   1 x 1.5

2 x 1   2 x 1

3 x 1   1 x 3

4 x 1   1 x 4

6 x 1   6 x 1

8 x 1   1 x 8

16 x 1   16 x 1

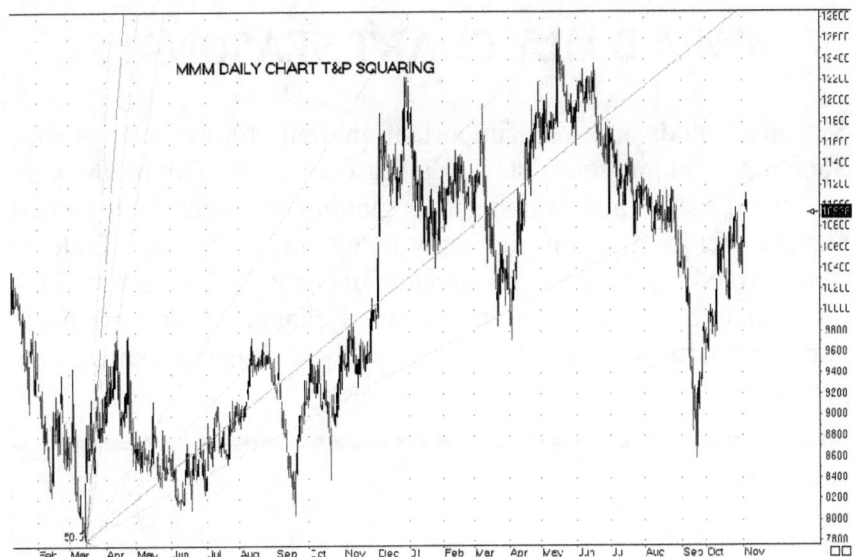

MMM DAILY CHART SEASONALS

Seasonal trends are very important in both futures and stocks. Sometimes major trends start at a seasonal point. Divide the year up into quarters and watch the beginning of each. In the chart pictured below it is amazing how many major tops and bottoms were formed after a quarterly division of the year. You should look for a change a trend with any seasonal change. If you are using intraday charts you should be aware of these seasonal change time periods.

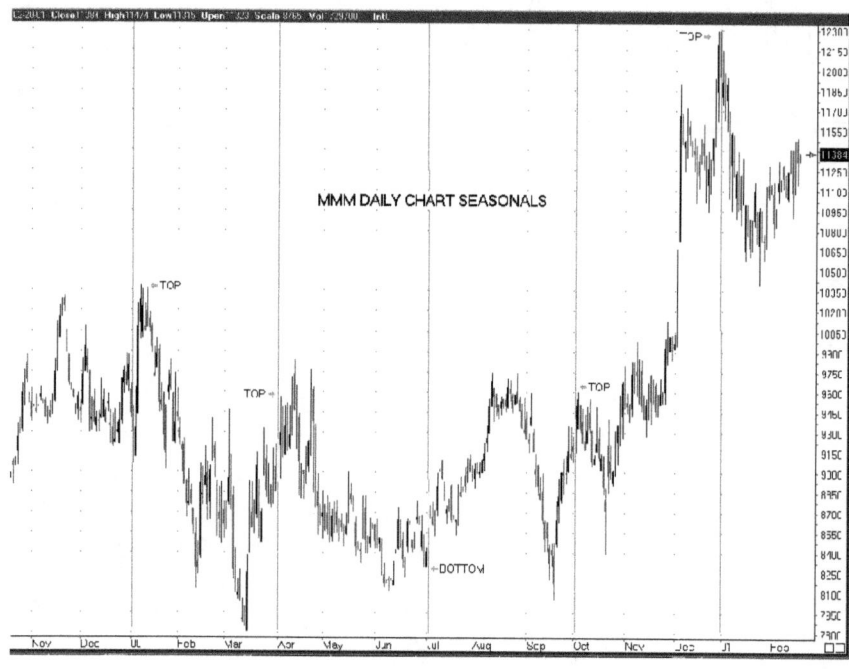

SQUARE OF NINE FIXED AND SEASONALS

The Square of Nine can be used along with the season chart. In many cases you will find that on a particular quarterly date that the price of the stock will be exactly in tune with the Square of Nine. The previous chart of MMM had several highs and lows exactly in tune with Cardinal and Fixed points of the Square of Nine chart.

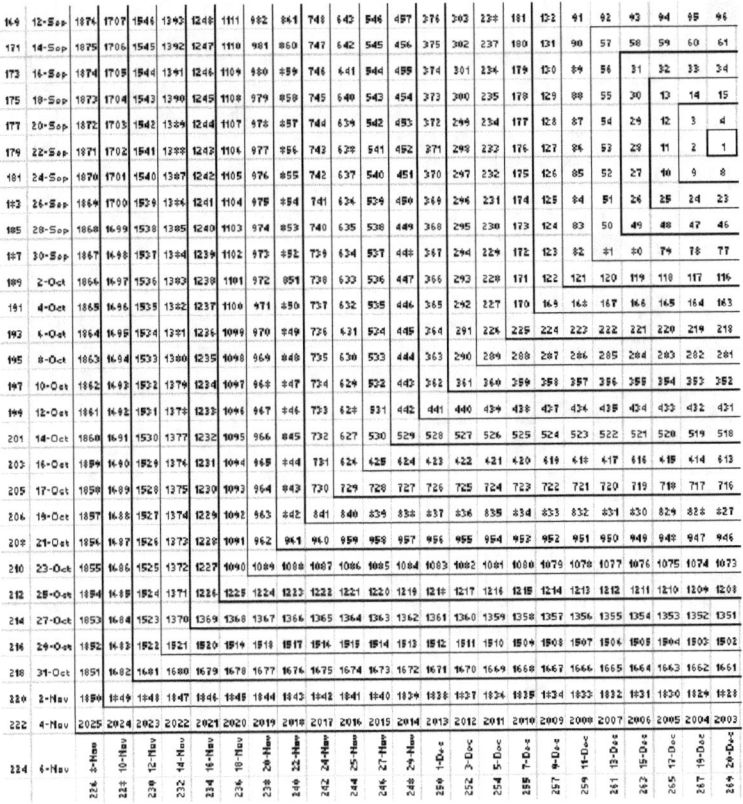

TXN 5-MIN CHART AND THE FIXED SQUARE OF NINE

The Fixed and the Cardinal Points on the Square of Nine are extremely important. The points on this chart hit exactly on these points. See the attached Square of Nine.

TXN 5-MIN CHART AND THE FIXED SQ OF NINE WITH CHANNELS

In this example we created parallel channels with the Fixed Square Points and the bottom at 29.70. When they reached the top at 31.60 it was a clear sale.

TXN 5-MIN FIXED SQ OF NINE WITH CHANNELS AND VARIABLE

In this example we have added the variable low of 30.00 to the chart. We paralleled the bottom with the first high to make a trading channel to the objective of 31.80, which was clearly made on the chart.

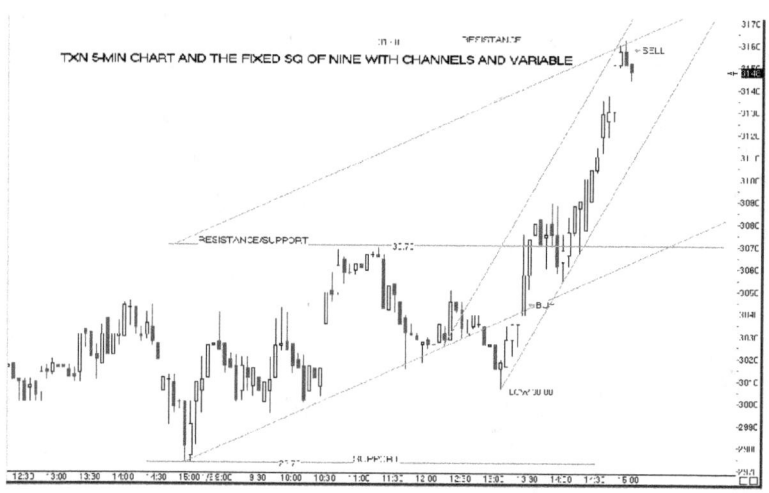

307	308	309	310	311	312	313	314	315	316	317	318	319	320	321	322	323	324	325
306	241	242	243	244	245	246	247	248	249	250	251	252	253	254	255	256	257	326
305	240	183	184	185	186	187	188	189	190	191	192	193	194	195	196	197	258	327
304	239	182	133	134	135	136	137	138	139	140	141	142	143	144	145	198	259	328
303	238	181	132	91	92	93	94	95	96	97	98	99	100	101	146	199	260	329
302	237	180	131	90	57	58	59	60	61	62	63	64	65	102	147	200	261	330
301	236	179	130	89	56	31	32	33	34	35	36	37	66	103	148	201	262	331
300	235	178	129	88	55	30	13	14	15	16	17	38	67	104	149	202	263	332
299	234	177	128	87	54	29	12	3	4	5	18	39	68	105	150	203	264	333
298	233	176	127	86	53	28	11	2	1	6	19	40	69	106	151	204	265	334
297	232	175	126	85	52	27	10	9	8	7	20	41	70	107	152	205	266	335
296	231	174	125	84	51	26	25	24	23	22	21	42	71	108	153	206	267	336
295	230	173	124	83	50	49	48	47	46	45	44	43	72	109	154	207	268	337
294	229	172	123	82	81	80	79	78	77	76	75	74	73	110	155	208	269	338
293	228	171	122	121	120	119	118	117	116	115	114	113	112	111	156	209	270	339
292	227	170	169	168	167	166	165	164	163	162	161	160	159	158	157	210	271	340
291	226	225	224	223	222	221	220	219	218	217	216	215	214	213	212	211	272	341
290	289	288	287	286	285	284	283	282	281	280	279	278	277	276	275	274	273	342
361	360	359	358	357	356	355	354	353	352	351	350	349	348	347	346	345	344	343

PYRAPOINT TOOL

Don Hall, a master Gann trader for over 30 years developed the Pyrapoint tool in Ensign for Windows. A book is available from Traders World called Pyrapoint for $150. It is well work the money. Don Hall also holds seminars on Pyrapoint trading. It consists of over 200 pages with the rules and many techniques to use this excellent tool. To order the book call Traders World at 800-288-4266. The next three articles are reprints from from Traders World Magazine on Pyrapoint Trading.

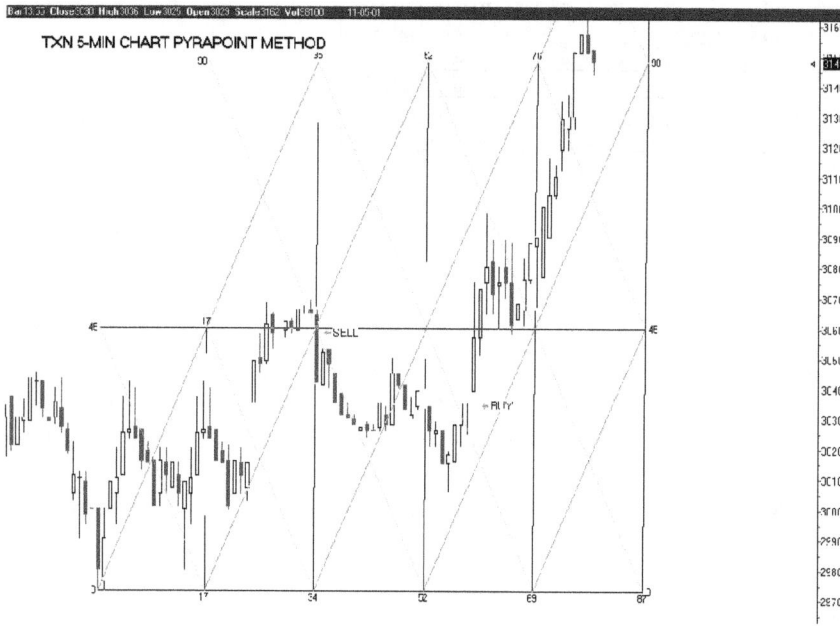

GANN'S SECRET PYTHAGOREAN SQUARE

By Don E. Hall

Many manuscripts and seminars have been presented regarding trading stocks, bonds, and commodities. Indeed, trading has a very unique and ancient history, dating back to the earliest recordings of any type of commerce.

No one will expound for long on the simplicity of the challenge; and again, no one denies that it is a mammoth challenge. The percentage of failures versus the percentages of triumphs will attest to this. It has been said that more people fail at this profession than most commercial businesses. It is also a known fact that the percentage ratio of wins to losses is definitely on the side of the losses.

Realizing this, some 40 years ago we set goals that we felt needed to be addressed (and indeed, answered) by any so-called trading system. From our earliest studies we defined our system needs to do at least the following:

1. Establish trend

2. Have mathematical and ongoing stop placement

3. Have realistic and accurate objectives in any move

4. Know mathematically when a move has started and when it is culminated

5. Know at all times -- in any trade -- where we are in our planned objective

6. Provide peace of mind to the trader to avert being ill with anxiety overnight or even during the day

To us this meant the graphic source of considerable information should be easily digested and interpreted.

TO US THIS SUGGESTED A SQUARE WITHIN THE PARAMETERS OF OUR CURRENT TRADING! We had not seen such a drawing available to us.

This led our studies toward Gann, Brenner, Bayer and Company.

When my father passed away in 1961 I recall that I was charting extensively -- and trading some.

I went through all of the stages from Point and Figure to Moving Averages, collected all the books on everyone's mailing list, it seemed, and then settled upon following the studies of a man who has shown us to be one of the most successful commodity traders of all time, Mr. W.D. Gann. This decision was supported by a fortunate event wherein I received the opportunity to retrace his path into Egypt and along the Nile.

History shows us that Mr. Gann made three trips abroad that were of significance to his studies: to England, to India and to Egypt.

He had one of the best history and data sources of the day, and much of this was acquired in English libraries and museums. We have studied much of this.

Second, he was known to be very astute in mathematical circles. Much of this credit has been attributed to his trips to India and places where, we are told, he studied a very unique and effective math system. This system has been compared to our earliest studies of what we now call "modern math." At any rate, he learned to use floating decimal procedures and he was very proficient in the use of numbers.

The third important trip abroad seemed to culminate, and indeed concentrate, in Egypt. Not as much seems to be known of these Egyptian studies. Our quest became to learn the objective of this particular phase of his studies. We believe that we have accomplished this. Certainly he rated along with the greats: Livermore, Brenner, Bayer, Barouch and others.

He was especially known for his commodity trading which was considered tougher than stocks because of the leverage.

From the early '60s when I began to study somewhat in earnest, and following at least to the mid-seventies, I attended many seminars, but I especially attempted to attend all seminars available on Gann.

Alas, however! I never found the secret as shown by his verified results.

It was only after attending most of the Gann seminars, administered by people all of whom were claiming to have his secret, that I came to the conclusion that there was a question as to whether the teachers were actually duplicating his record. Indeed, they were usually not even in fair range of his results.

It was then that I began dissecting his seminars and assimilating certain segments of different seminars. I came to some conclusions, not the least of which was, in my opinion:

THAT HE WASN'T ALWAYS TEACHING THAT WHICH HE WAS ACTUALLY TRADING.

I can stand corrected, but the next ten years proved to me the validity of my convictions. Mr. Gann indicated that he would not reveal the true secret of the math involved. However, he also indicated that if one were to spend the time which he had (25 years) and covered the material at least three times, that it could be revealed to a serious student. I have qualified for the years, plus some -- sometimes to the exhaustion of my family, I'm sure.

I SUBMIT TO YOU THAT THE PYRAPOINT SYSTEM IS THE PRINCIPLE THAT HE USED. We can prove it, I feel. But if you will accept our point, in our book we intend to spend our time with "hands-on" proof so that we can learn the true and full potential of the system. This is why we go to a seminar and why we study the manual. Incidentally, we should have no copyright infringements because, to our knowledge and research, Mr. Gann never taught this in any of his seminars, even to his associate, who I had the privilege to personally know for some seven years, Mr. Renato Alghini. "Reno" was with Gann for six years, actually sharing close trading desks. Reno confirmed the extremely private personality of his friend. This is shown in most of Gann's writings and seminars.

Reno passed away a few years ago. However, during the author's years of acquaintance with him, he shared a few facts that made the direction of our efforts truly appear validated. One of the confirmation factors seemed especially worthwhile in the revelation that Gann carried a small paper in hand when in the "pit" for his most successfully recorded trades. This paper, Reno related, was a miniature Pythagorean Cube. One more reason to believe that we had to unravel this mystic marvel -- and that we were, indeed, on the right track for trading understanding.

Mr. Gann died in 1956.

It is significant to note that a favorite statement of Gann serves us well when we state that we believe that EVERY TOP AND EVERY BOTTOM in the markets have a CALCULABLE counterpart -- a formula for projections and targets for both PRICE and for TIME. His quotes included that of the noted mathematician Faraday. Mr. Gann said, "If we wish to avert failure in speculation, we must deal with causes. Everything in existence is based on exact proportion and perfect relationship. There is no chance in nature, because mathematical principles of the highest order lie at the foundation of all things." Faraday said: "There is nothing in the Universe but mathematical points of force."

THIS IS THE TRUE BASIS OF THE PYRAPOINT SYSTEM OF TRADING.

Although we give full credit to Gann, Wycoff, Brenner, Jenson, Bayer and other contemporaries of earlier times for their contributions to mathematical approaches to the markets, we must tell you that this is likely not what was being sold in $5000 seminars. We sincerely believe that PYRAPOINT is what they so successfully traded.

Gann and Company reportedly used many "squares" -- the more important often included such numbers as 3, 4, 12, 15, 24, 45, 72, 90, 144, 180 and 360, we are told. Gann has been quoted as saying that one must compute TIME, based upon PRICE.

THIS WE DO.

Gann also is reported to have indicated that PRICE must be seen or projected upon a circle -- then he said that the circle had to be squared to obtain the TIME for trend changes in the market.

THIS WE ALSO DO.

Although we have enlisted the assistance of a programmer to place PYRAPOINT on the Tradestation format, it is easy to hand-draw and hand-calculate when all data is in place. A number of variations of the Pythagorean Cube are available. We have used the format as used by Forrest Wilke of Lincoln, Nebraska, in his version of the "Square of Nine Gann Wheel."

Relative to the charting technique, we acknowledge two specific factors that will assist your learning process: (1) Since our approach to charting is presented as Universal, it is obvious that more than one lesson should show on a chart. It should be ongoing. Thus we can show repetitive charts with an additional lesson blending into the sister chart. (2) Since you will be examining specific entry/exit and other finite points of interest, you may find that an "exploded view" may, at times, better serve you to clarify the total picture so that you can place it into the larger picture -- a larger degree, if you will. Although no emphasis is placed upon the supporting momentum charts that we use from time to time, we do sometimes apply inputs that we consider to be compatible to PYRAPOINT. This should not materially change your understanding or your learning of the study.

The derivative of the PYRAPOINT system is the result of our experience of some 35 years, wherein we have tried all of the systems which are likely in your portfolio as well, discarding and trying again, until finally coming to the conclusion that we would need to clear out the massive amounts of underbrush (and there are piles of it) -- and to see if core data didn't have some common thread. It is our opinion that we have, indeed, found the Universal Thread. Heard that one before? Read it in an article (or a hundred or so) perhaps?

BUT READ ON -- WE PROMISE YOU MORE POTENTIAL

THAN YOU ARE USED TO RECEIVING.

First, let us examine some of the background and origins of our compiled data that essentially makes up a majority of our CORE DATA.

Part is taken from the lessons that I feel that W.D. Gann learned while in Egypt, and specifically in the study of the Great Pyramid, and its dimensions. Part is the Universal Golden Ratio, but used in a CALCULATED manner to make up the Gann-Type Squares. It is the study of this that brings us to core data that we will use. The heart of the whole system depends upon a calculation and the interpretation of the Gann "Square of Nine." This likely goes back to Brenner, Bayer, Gann, and eventually back to the real core in the Pythagorean Cube (as well as the early Egyptian Calendar, we are told).

To answer as to the history of the PYRAPOINT Trading System, we need to start with the core data and the core authors. To do this, we begin with Pythagoras who lived, as did Socrates, a few hundred years +/-, A.D.

Some historians tell us that Pythagoras, like Socrates, was guilty of teaching the common man in early Greece. We say "guilty" because Socrates got the Hemlock juice for teaching outside of the Priesthood. Since this was the primary manner of control for the hierarchy, they naturally frowned upon this type of teaching. Thus it was, we are told, that Pythagoras took exile to Egypt where he stayed 22 years -- the time it took to complete the Priesthood.

Is it any wonder that the "father of our mathematics" (especially the geometric math) was able to bring back to Greece all that he learned in the "cradle of mathematical civilization" of that day? It included such things as that which we base our system upon even today. Mr. Gann learned this from his trip to Egypt, in our opinion, because at the top of the learning list were our vital and basic tools -- the square, the circle and the Hypotenuse Rule. These: Phi, Pi, Square Root, and squaring of a number are addressed later for your application in your understanding of the PYRAPOINT Trading System. This "revelation" given by Pythagoras in the first few centuries A.D. is still Universally accepted, and it is evident from the smallest snail, through the life and body of man and plant, through the Milky Way. This is an ever onward, ever outward process, and is indeed in the markets as well. The learning of this process is at the core of our learning system.

One last passing observation: the tools to which we referred as primary in the marketplace, and indeed in our PYRAPOINT System of Trading, are found in the Great Pyramid of Giza which was built 2500 years before Pythagoras. Doesn't it make one wonder what took place in that 2500 years since all of the above-mentioned tools are evident in the Pyramids and the tombs? It is our conclusion that Gann had to realize this from his personal trips to Egypt, as the author personally did when in Cairo and associated areas that he had the privilege to study, in the area all along the Nile River. This included the quarries where some granite was perfectly formed to Phi proportions, evident in the manner of relationship of the height to base, and which are reported to weigh literally tons.

We have avoided inclusion of many of the very fascinating theories advanced by the Egyptians themselves relative to the Great Pyramid. In passing, let us say that we have relayed to you only the things which relate to the markets, and which we have had the privilege of observations and determination.

Worthy of mention are a couple of theories advanced by a college-educated contact (the author's guide during his stay in Egypt) especially as related to the Great Pyramid:

(1) The limestone-clad granite structure covering 13 acres and extending more than 450' in height is credited with carrying very exacting dimensions. An early Egyptian mathematical index, which they used, accurately projects the distance to the sun (from its height), the mass of the earth (from its mass), and the circumference of the earth at its largest mile (from its perimeter).

(2) Mummification seems a characteristic of the Pyramid -- not found outside.

Without question, we are studying results of universally prime information -- and we can show you that it is primary (and indeed the key) to the markets.

Our question has been how should this learning be best conducted in the manual?

Our answer to you: in the simplest, most straightforward manner that we can, to get you to be able to USE the System. This will be a hands-on trading system/study -- you must be able to use the information, even if you have to accept some information for later proof. Our plan is to present to you the schedule of information which you need for this learning process. We will not dwell on the process so that we might spend productive time in the "hands-on" role with actual charts (complete with commentary and instructions.) We believe that this is where the true worth of any system is weighed. It is our opinion that it must be used effectively, and in first person, for one to get a full appreciation of just how real and how consistent potential returns can be with this system. The charts will truly act as 1000 words. It is our intent to call your attention to basic "setups" in many different topics of various trading subjects and of various time frames as well. This will assist you in learning the UNIVERSALITY as well as FLEXIBILITY of PYRAPOINT.

To use the PYRAPOINT technique, please realize that we are not asking that you discard any of your learned good trading rules. We do ask that, since we are operating on a totally calculated line and square, that you follow what we have learned to be a very highly accurate set of simple rules. The nice part of this technique is that it can overlay any theory or system that may presently be of interest or in use by you. Even if you choose not to use PYRAPOINT as your primary theorem, please look at the rules and squares for confirmation. WE ARE BETTING THAT YOU WILL CHANGE YOUR PRIMARY UNIT!

The rules which we use are self-evident on your chart of the square for the price parameter in which your commodity or stock is trading. We operate upon the theory that if we can successfully trade the square representing the parameter currently trading then, in all probability, we will have success in the next square as well. Thus, the rules that we submit for this square will be universally acceptable for any commodity or stock that you will be trading.

The only preface which we caution is to fit the TIME unit and the PRICE unit into scales that are "common sense" to the parameters of price and volatility. In other words, use a square size that will reflect the manner in which the unit is trading. One way of confirming this "common sense" is to realize that it would take a considerably smaller square to reflect the action of an hourly chart of a low-volatility commodity or stock than it would take for a daily or even a weekly, especially in high-volatility status. Again, this should not be a primary worry for you. PYRAPOINT and your own judgment will suffice as soon as you become acquainted. Actually, you can see the picture with very little experience. The worst scenario that you might have is working with a square that is within a square. It is all repetitive, "ever onward, ever outward." You are simply the recorder of a very Universal and Wonderful Law. As soon as you have the ability to build a square from data provided to you, then you are ready to find out what all of these lines really represent. All of this is governed by six simple and totally defined rules.

Given the nature and complexity of trading, we need to KNOW WHERE WE ARE AT A GIVEN TIME, WHAT WE SHOULD EXPECT AS A MODE FOR EACH PRICE LEVEL, AND WHAT TO DO WHEN IT CHANGES -- and it will change!! Just be ready!!

Technical trading has been referenced to trend lines or trading lines, which make up a parameter for rules of trading. PYRAPOINT is no different in that particular regard. Therefore, we have set upon a path or plan to define these lines, establish the parameters, define the parameters, and then to provide the reasoning behind the rules which make up

PYRAPOINT's system -- just as other systems which you have studied. What is different in the study is the CALCULATION and its methodology, and the rules for application within each of the parameters of each square.

These are some of the studies/theorems which Pythagorous brought back to Greece and which are covered to make PYRAPOINT valid:

(1) Tools of the PYRAPOINT System are found in The Great Pyramid -- as are tools of the circle. They include:

a. Pi

b. Phi

c. Square Root

d. Square of Number

e. Hypotenuse Rule

(2) Pythagorean Cube is the core of the PYRAPOINT System of Trading.

(3) PYRAPOINT unveils mysteries of the Pythagorean Cube -- the Square of Nine --

Egyptian Calendar.

(4) PYRAPOINT interprets moves of the markets as reflected on the "P.C."

(5) PYRAPOINT identifies calculated squares for every parameter of price.

(6) PYRAPOINT lets you graphically know where to enter (whether buying or selling) and gives the highway to travel to maintain the position profitably.

(7) PYRAPOINT tells you when to expect a trend change, gives you the objective

both long and short until the time frame and beyond.

(8) PYRAPOINT gives you the exact action per your position in the calculated square at any, and at all times.

(9) The Trading System works in all denominations of time frames, allowing you to

confirm as well as plan. PYRAPOINT also allows all time frames to be correlated into reasonable and profitable squares -- even with small/large price ranges or small/large time frames.

(10) PYRAPOINT operates on the mathematical information that every top and every bottom has a mathematical counterpart -- and herein lies the opportunity to project the action of the market -- and to profit therefrom.

(11) The System unlocks the relationship of PRICE and TIME and squares them on a 360 degree circle for each move.

At this juncture, it would seem that the all-important Pythagorean Cube (the "P.C.") should be further described. You will note that a sample of the tool is provided. It is shown as a number series, beginning with number 1 in the center, and progressing ever-onward and ever-outward in a spiral of spaces in sequence. It also has the characteristic that it is divided evenly in fourths, eighths, sixteenths, etc., as the numbers progress in the circle.

In the "P.C.'s" pure state, before any added divisions, it is reported to be a calendar as used by early Egyptians. We personally find this to be a very interesting synopsis since it, too, would date back far earlier than the celebrated works of Pythagoras.

One of the things we do know about the Egyptians' early use of the "P.C." is that it was used in their mathematical teachings and usage. IT IS AN UNERRING CALCULATOR IN THE WORK TO WHICH WE APPLY IT.

The "P.C." was further refined by scholars such as W.D. Gann (and likely Brenner, Bayer and others) for use in calculating trading strategies. Since Gann, for instance, made his famous studies and seminars around the establishment of PRICE and TIME as projected on a circle, it follows that this tool would lend itself to circular measurement and, indeed, fractions thereof. Gann called this "P.C." a MASTER CALCULATOR for his famous work.

To use the calculator to its fullest support level in their calculations, scholars such as Gann have divided the circle as applied by the "P.C." into divisions of the 360° circle which it depicts. They have also given TIME as well as PRICE divisions or sections as shown in this calculator.

GANN'S ROAD MAP APPROACH

By Don E. Hall

Probably no one in the trading world has received more discussion than W.D. Gann. Discussions of the famous trader have ranged from awe and admiration to downright disbelief. Some of us found this to be one of the foundation bricks of reason for studying his complex trading life. Having been in the markets in both cash and futures since the mid 1950s, it became evident to me that not all of the information, which I found to be touted even in those early days was 100%. This is no surprise to most of you as readers of a technical source such as Traders World. More than a surprise, I found it to be a challenge.

The percentage of correct trades attributable to Mr. Gann just did not fit the pattern, which was my lot in my own hedging and trading. Thus I set my goal to first find out as much as I could as to the validity of the claims. My acquaintance and friendship with Mr. "Reno" Alghini, a friend and close trading associate of Mr. Gann, started me in earnest to the next goal. It also gave me the road map of my next challenge.

Reno often commented that when Gann went to the pit, he always carried the Pythagorean Cube (Square of Nine as we know it), and many times, nothing else for support. This fact made me realize that I had my work assignment.

Gann's record in public and under scrutiny made one conclusion evident to me: it just had to be simpler than that to which I had been exposed in books, seminars, and courses – just had to be!

From this point in my studies, roughly halfway through the 45 years which I have determined this market interest, I began Gann studies in nearly 100% of my efforts. The reason: no one to whom I had knowledge had done so well in trading, nor nearly so consistently. If one needs a guide to hang his or her goals upon, in my opinion, it is CONSISTENCY. Even with his high percentage of accuracy, we are shown that Gann still maintained a very good ratio of dollars earned per trade – and he apparently did so with a minimum of risk. This meant one thing to me: he had to know what he was trading, when to trade it, when to be dormant to a trade, and at what point to be in and/or get out. It seems to me that these are worthy goals with which to trade by any standards. Thus our quest for more and more information on the Pythagorean Cube seemed to be justified. After all, if it were the tool that it seemed to be when Gann was under fire by the press as well as in the pit, why then should it not be worthy of our 100% effort? It was and is. Thus the birth of PYRAPOINT: A Trade Analogy.

Just what is this system called PYRAPOINT: A Trade Analogy? In the simplest of terms, it is the unraveling of the Pythagorean Cube.

As we have stated in an earlier article, we likely aren't the first to see the almost mystic market waves and, indeed, the full moves as they relate to the Pythagorean Cube.

PYRAPOINT: A Trade Analogy simply gives us a plan to use these wonderful moves, and a place to get (or stay) out of a loss or losses.

The important word in the prior paragraph is "SIMPLY." No system or plan is of much use to us, in our opinion, if it involves so much effort and research per trade that we cannot ACT on the recommendation. The market moves much too quickly for very involved criteria. It is our belief that Gann did not have that much time either, as determined by the number of trades credited to his per-hour of trading.

We are convinced that one needs a system that provides early and continuing indications of market action. We believe that one needs a road map approach. We are also convinced that this recognizable direction must be familiar enough to us for our action without hesitation. Confidence – right? Herein lies the true basis for discipline, that all-important factor for successful trading. We need to see the opportunity, read it for target and for time – then act. Call it confidence – call it discipline – it is the answer to successful trades – simply and quickly. We don't even necessarily require a computer if we have the chart of question and recognize the "stop and go lights."

So the plot thickens as to reasons for unraveling the Pythagorean Cube.

We are happy to report that our serious students have found our teachings in PYRAPOINT: A Trade Analogy to yield to them a better trading life. Some have graciously given us a "best" rating. The single-most heard praise is that it simply makes sense – that it yields a reason for our position of entry and exit – that it gives a track to follow for full fruition of a trade – and that (if we follow the six simple rules) we simply do have a better bottom line. We believe that this is what it is all about!

This doesn't mean that our grade card does not indicate that we haven't experienced the "normal 3%" who aren't claiming to be in this group. We not only understand this, we anticipate some reluctance to read or study 300 pages (especially with so much information "out there" today). Our comment however is to recall that nearly half of the pages are pictures (charts). We expect to confirm all of our text. This is a workbook of knowledge for your better trading. It is to show you what is actually going on in this world of trading via the Pythagorean Cube. It is not to place on the mantel as décor. Actually our students relate that it is revealing to other fields as well – but certainly the markets.

It has been said that it seems like a lot of information to learn the "Square of Nine." I hear you. I tried it for 20 years. Friend, if you have learned the art and calculations of the mystic diagonals, where to place your entries and exits, where to expect changes (which direction and how much), how to regulate your squares for calculation, and then have developed good rules to control your marketing and your discipline – then I agree with you. I just haven't met a person who could show me these things. I am certain that this or these person(s) exist – otherwise I would undoubtedly not have found it to share. One last item for this topic: we have offered to answer your questions relative to our interpretations to assist you for a period of six months in the FAQ on our site. We care, and we want to answer your concerns.

As stated in the book, PYRAPOINT: A Trade Analogy, we have other reasons why we feel that it is truly "the answer" for most of us. The Pythagorean Cube and Theories are of much earlier origins than Pythagoras' discoveries brought back to Greece from his trek to Egypt. In fact, they are evident in the Great Pyramid and other architecture dating back to 2500 B.C. And as stated the book, it does make one wonder what really took place in that 2000 plus years era, since Pythagoras brought it to the Greeks in the first millennium A.D. It is from here that we began our education in the "modern sense" by the teachings of Pythagoras, sometimes referred to as the "father of modern mathematics" – especially trigonometry, algebraic equations of floating decimals, etc.

At this point let us emphasize that Gann was a particularly good mathematician. This was another clue to our further quest for answers as to how he was so accomplished. His research was quite extensive, even to countries besides Egypt, but he had this all behind him when under fire in the pit, and apparently relied heavily on the notorious Pythagorean Cube. It had to be basic – and it is. It had to be simple – and it is. It had to be accurate for both price and time – and it is. Above all, it had to be far more accessible and more rapidly understood than most of the complicated endeavors to which he is credited. Think about it! How much of what you see attributed to his success in the trading pit could he have done without multiple tools of assistance?

Personally, I have no problem with any of the interpretations of the many varieties of methodologies concerning W.D. Gann. My hat is off to many scholars as they have unwound fact after fact from his work. My point in this discussion is that there are dozens of productions of theories on his methodology, ranging from math to astrology, with many combinations – and with merit for the most part. The problem that I do have in my years of study is two-fold: (1) to assimilate a profitable trading plan from all of my books and papers which I have collected for two or three decades, as they relate to Gann's works and teachings, and (2) to sort all of the mass of information into a simple and usable plan for trading.

Again, I believe that Gann did his analogy for a trade quickly and accurately with tools which, were available to him at the moment of truth – the moment to ACT on a given trade. And, again, it just had to be simpler than most Gann presentations of the day. In our opinion, the answer is Universality, ease of understanding and of interpretation, speed of determination and action, accuracy in all of these factors – the answer is SIMPLICITY. The answer is the unraveling of the Pythagorean Cube in a manner that will allow us PEACE OF MIND AND PROFIT, while not overfeeding our margin account. Mr. Gann was right: the answer is to KNOW your trade. In our opinion, this means to KNOW IT ON THE PYTHAGOREAN CUBE. Believe us – like the carpenter's square, there is a world of education on this 4500-year-old Pythagorean Cube. We must learn to use it to prosper! As the readers of PYRAPOINT: A Trade Analogy have stated, "we must stay on the diagonal highways that the Pythagorean Cube undeniably provides – calculate the squares (the posts) and the fence is there for us" – SIMPLY!

PYRAPOINT TIME AND PRICE

By Howard Arrington

This is another reprinted article from Traders World Magazine concerning the Pyrapoint system.

William D. Gann (1878-1955) was a legendary trader who designed several unique techniques for analyzing price charts. He developed a unique combination of precise mathematical and geometric principles, which are not easy to grasp. Gann analysts have spent years pouring over old charts and writings in search of Gann's secret, and there is no end to the number of people who claim to have discovered Gann's insight and technique that has eluded everyone else. Perhaps someone has discovered it. I am not in a position to appraise all the claims because I am not a Gann expert and have not read Gann's writings.

Don Hall has published a book and developed a system called Pyrapoint, which seems to me to be well founded in Gann principles. The purpose of this article is to take one idea used in Don's work, and present it from a different approach, and yet arrive at the same useful conclusion. I hope even Don will find my article to be an original insight to substantiate the validity of his work.

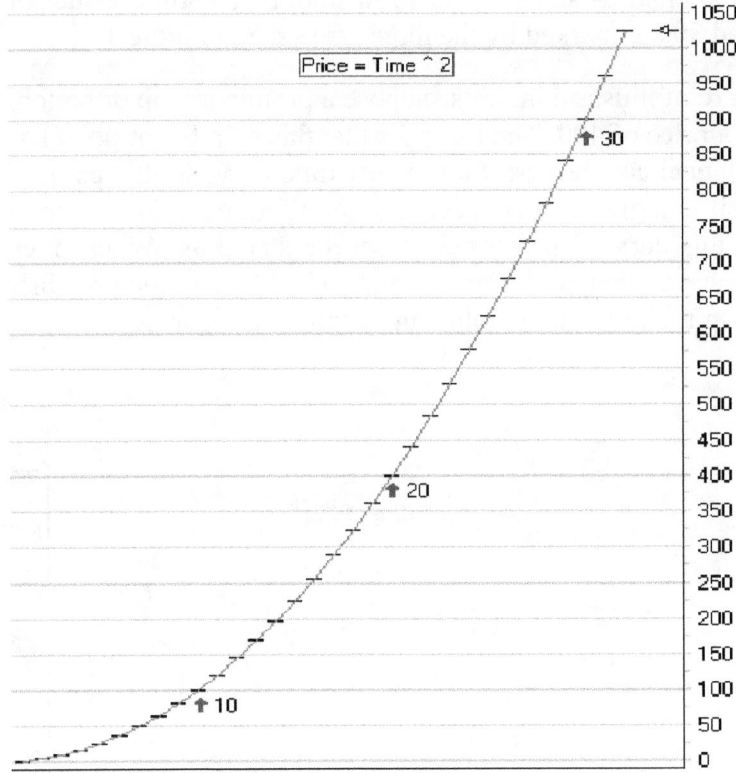

Figure 1

Gann's geometric angles are trend lines drawn from prominent tops or bottoms at certain angles. The most important angle is 45 degrees, which means the line's slope is one unit of price per unit of time. (Note: Depending of the chart scale used, the line may or may not appear to be plotted at a 45-degree angle.) For years, I thought this is what Gann analysts meant by the phrase 'squaring time and price.' However, Don's Pyrapoint method gave me a new insight, which is:

Price = Time squared or $P = t^2$

Let me take this mathematical relationship and develop it in this article. The above relationship between price and time can be plotted on a chart as shown in this illustration. The time values of 10, 20, and 30 are marked by the three arrows. See Figure 1.

For the sake of illustration, let's suppose a prominent top or bottom occurs at a price of 400. The theory is that this significant point has a mathematical counterpart. Start a new time curve at this point in time, and it will give us an expectation for a future top or bottom to occur on this curve. This principle can be stated as 'When price meets time, a change is imminent.' This 'price meets time' relationship is shown in the following chart. See Figure 2.

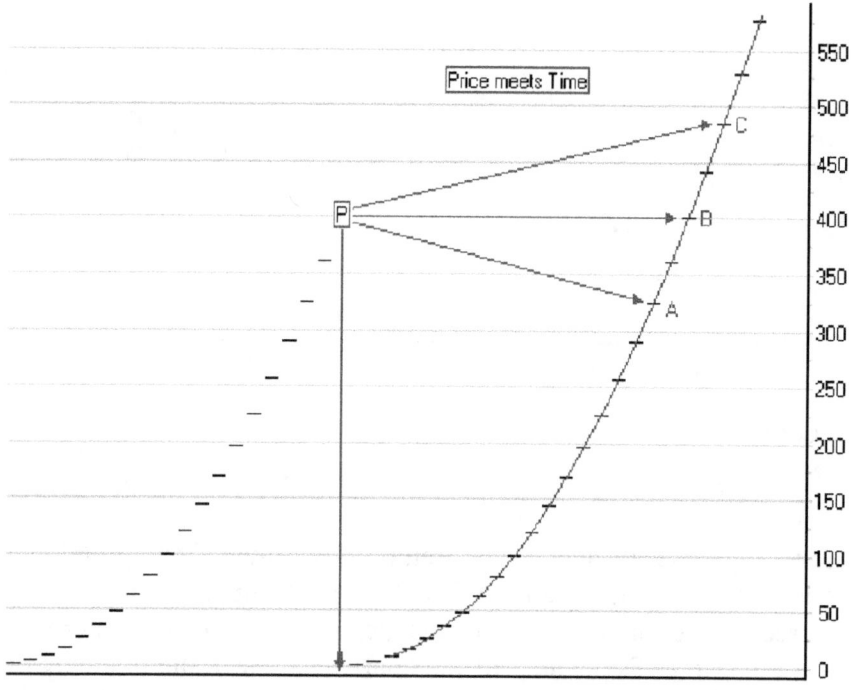

Figure 2

With the prominent top or bottom at P, if price meets the curve at point A it will do so in 18 bars. The time to A is the square root of the price at A. Price at A is 324. Square root of 324 is 18.

If price meets the curve at point B, it will do so in 20 bars. The time to B is the square root of the price at B. Price at B is 400, therefore the time to B is 20 bars.

If price meets the curve at point C, it will do so in 22 bars. This is a very interesting concept! Remember that price and time are related by the formula: $P = t^2$ or $t = sqrt(P)$ In this article, I will develop the mathematics for the slope of a trend line using the price and time relationship presented in the previous article. Let's work with the model illustrated in this See Figure 3.

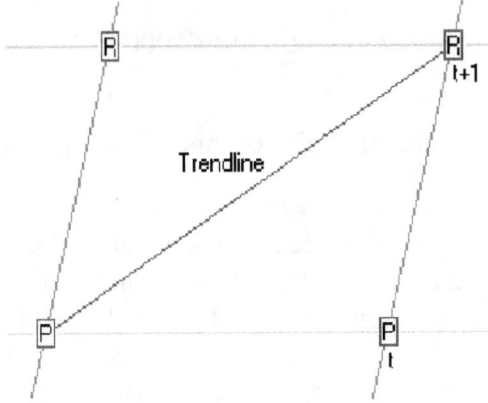

Figure 3

From the previous article, the next time curve will be t bars away for a given price P. At a time t+1 price would meet the curve at price P1. Now, lets solve for the slope of the trend line shown in blue, which connects P and P1.

$P = t^2$

$P1 = (t + 1)^2 = t^2 + 2t + 1 = P + 2t + 1$

Slope = (Change in price) / (Change in time)

Change in price = P1 - P = P + 2 t + 1 - P = 2 t + 1 = 2 t + 2 - 1 = 2 [t + 1] - 1

Change in time = t + 1

Therefore, slope of P to P1 is = (2 [t + 1] - 1) / (t+1) = 2 - 1 / (t+1)

$= 2 - 1 / \text{sqrt}(P1)$

If we normalize all prices to consider three significant digits, then all prices will fall in the range of [100 ... 1000]. By substituting the price boundaries into the slope formula, we can get a range of slopes as follows.

For a P1 of 100, the slope of the up trend line to $100 = 2 - 1 / 10 = 1.9$

For a P1 of 1000, the slope of the up trend line to $1000 = 2 - 1 / 100 = 1.99$

The slope of the up trend line at the midpoint of this price range is $2 - 1 / \text{sqrt}(500) = 1.96$

Let's call this trend line a 45-degree line because we developed the slope using one unit of price change from P to P1 with one unit of time t. For this 45-degree line, the slope is basically 2. I think this is strong justification as to why Gann used 2 cents as the price grid interval of his daily grain charts. Such a scale layout would naturally give Gann 45 degree angles with a slope of 2 cents per daily bar. I have shown that 2 is the slope of the upward 45 degree trend line that develops from the price and time relationship given by the formula: $P = t \wedge 2$.

One can solve for the slope of the downward trend line from P1 to P to obtain this result:

Slope of P1 to $P = (-2 t - 1) / (t-1) = (-2 [t - 1] - 3) / (t-1) = -2 - 3 / (t-1) = -2 - 3 / (\text{sqrt}(P) - 1)$

For a P of 100, the slope of the down trend line to $100 = -2 - 3/9 = -2.33$

For a P of 1000, the slope of the down trend line to $1000 = -2 - 3/99 = -2.03$

Again, the slope of the down trend line approaches a value of -2. Therefore, -2 is a good approximation for the slope of a downward 45-degree trend line.

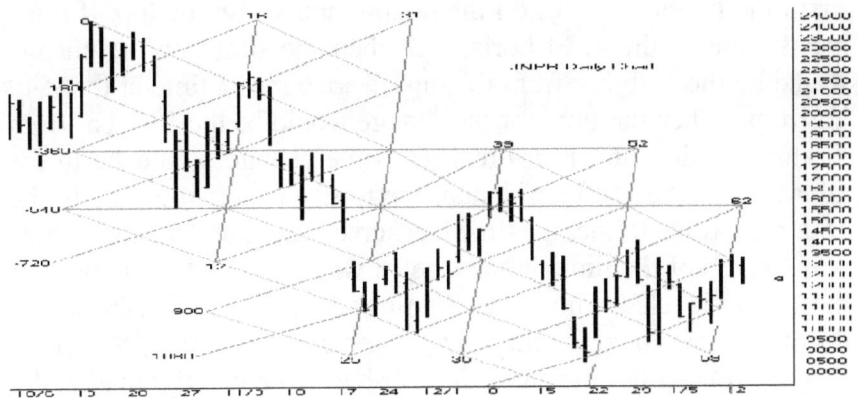

Now I would not bother to give you the mathematics in the previous two articles if I did not find application of this theory in the charts. I used the mathematics given in the first two articles to develop a tool in ESPL, which, draws horizontal lines at calculated price levels, and nearly vertical time curves at the calculated time intervals. This forms a grid of trapezoids like the previous illustration. (Don Hall calls them 'squares'.) Diagonal lines connect the corners of the trapezoids to give support and resistance trend lines. Here is a daily chart of JNPR with the construction started on the highest high. All price levels, time intervals, and trend lines are constructed mathematically from two pieces of information: the price $244.50 on the date 10-16-2000.

There is more in this chart than I have space to explain. But, I can point out some characteristics. The horizontal price lines have a label on the left, which is a degree of rotation around a Square of 9. This is covered in the Pyrapoint book, but is beyond the scope of this article. Note that in my example, the time lines are nearly vertical. This is a slight variation from the method of construction in the Pyrapoint book, which shows vertical lines. I feel that my presentation is appropriate because of the theory of the time curve illustrated in my first article. The time curve forms the left and right sides of the trapezoid, and the price levels form the top and bottom sides.

Time: Time is measured by the time curve, which is related to price. Tip: 'As price meets time, a change is imminent.' Note the first time line labeled 12 on the bottom and 16 on the top. If price meets time at the -720 horizontal, then the time for the change would be the 12th bar from the top. If price meets time at the -540 horizontal, then the time for the change would be the 13th bar from the top. At the -360 horizontal, the time change would be in the 14th bar. At the -180 horizontal, the time change would be in the 15th bar. At the 0 line, the time measured would be 16 bars. That is why the top of the time line is labeled with a 16, and the bottom of the line is labeled with a 12. Starting at 16, for each 180 degree down the time count is reduced by one bar, or for every 180 degree rise, the time count increases another bar. Note that the market did experience a change when price met the time curve labeled 12 to 16!

The price at the 12 to 16-time line was used to obtain a forecast of the 2nd time line, which is labeled 25 to 31. As the price meets each time curve, a new time curve is calculated based on the price. Each of the time curves shows excellent correlation with market change when price met the time line.

Prices: The prominent high of $24.50 is the calculation basis for all the horizontal price levels that are shown. Tip: The market seeks out these price levels, and you can calculate these prices in advance. Note how the market fell to the -540 horizontal, rallied to the -180 horizontal, fell to the -900 level, rallied to the -540 level, fell to the -1080 level, and rallied to the -720 level.

Trend Lines: The downward 45-degree trend lines shown in red create a flow channel, or 'price highway' as Don calls it. The upward 45-degree trend lines shown in green create a price highway going the other direction. The red lines are resistance lines that the market must close above to change direction from bearish to bullish. The green lines are support lines that the market must close below to change direction from bullish to bearish. We all have used upward trend lines placed underneath action lows to indicate support, and downward trend lines placed above action highs to indicate resistance. The beauty of this tool is that these diagonal trend lines are computed in advance, and the market seems to have respect for them. Price flows up and down the channels. The more you study the example, the more impressed I think you will be with this tool.

The Pyrapoint tool can also be applied to intra-day charts with good success. The size of the price interval used on a daily chart seems to be too big for use on an intra-day chart. No problem. Don points out that there are squares within a square. All one needs to do is sub-divided the price interval into halves, fourths, or eighths. The time interval is determined from price and will not change.

One question that I have dealt with is this: If the time interval computes to be 11 bars because the price is at 121, which intra-day bar time frame should I use?

If 1-minute bars are used, then we have a time curve 11 minutes later. If 2-minute bars are used, then the time curve would be 22 minutes later. If 5-minute bars are used, then the time curve is plotted 55 minutes later. Now do you see why I have a question? The selection of the intra-day bar time frame greatly affects the time interval measured by the next time curve.

Here is how I tackled the problem, and the proposed solution. I displayed a 1-minute chart and used a cycle tool to measure in hindsight the cycle rhythm from bottoms to bottoms, tops to tops, and/or bottoms to tops. When I found a cycle width that seems to fit by catching multiple turning points, I note the number of minutes in the cycle. I use this formula to estimate a good intra-day time frame to use.

Intra-day Bar Time Frame = Cycle width in minutes / sqrt(P)

Example: On the JNPR 1-minute chart I found a 65-minute cycle when the price was around \$133. Therefore, bar time = 65 / sqrt(133) = 5.6 minutes per bar. So, using a 6-minute chart, or possibly a 5-minute chart should show a good fit with the Pyrapoint tool. I happened to have been following a 5-minute chart, and I do find excellent correlation. I have used a smaller price interval by subdividing the 180-degree interval into eighths in this example. See Figure 5.

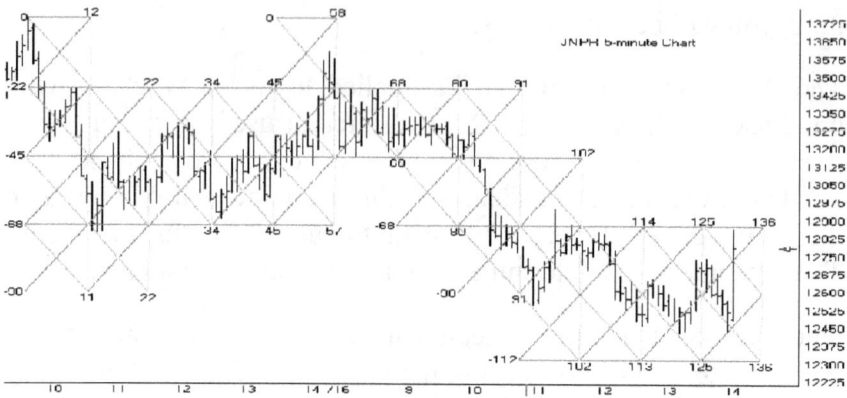
Figure 5

Please study the chart, and observe the flow of prices in the up and down trend channels. Note how trend changes occur on or near the vertical time curves, and how the market seeks the horizontal price levels. This entire road map is computed in advance from the prominent top that occurred on January 12th at 9:35 a.m.

CHART PATTERNS

There are many chart patterns that work hand and hand with the Elliott Wave Theory. It's a matter of training your eyes for pattern recognition and putting together Gann time and price analysis and the Elliott Wave theory. Many of the patterns by themselves give you the direction of the market. The following will give you most of the patterns that occur intraday in real time trading.

Most of the patterns were found in just the last few years. Astute market technicians who poured over thousands of charts found them. They were unknown to Gann. Go over the patterns and study them in relation to Gann Elliott Wave techniques. You'll find that the patterns work amazingly well.

You should also try to recognize these patterns on past data. Keep practicing until you can clearly see the patterns. Then you need to practice on recognizing these patterns on real-time date. That means recognizing the patterns on 5, 15, 30, 60-minute and daily charts. Anyone can recognize patterns and even Elliott Wave patterns on past charts. The real need is to recognize the patterns on real-time charts as the data is coming in.

TXN 5-MIN CHART BROADENING BOTTOM

The following chart illustrates the bullish broadening bottom formation. It starts out at an apex and broadens. Inside the broadening triangle is usually a 5-wave pattern. It finally breaks out in a 5-wave uptrend. In this case the last wave was the largest.

Strategy is to buy the reaction after the breakout and sell out at the top of the fifth wave.

TXN 5-MIN CHART RIGHT ANGLE BROADENING FORMATION

The Right Angle Broadening Formation is bearish. There is usually an ABC inside the formation and after the breakout a 5 wave down pattern. You short the breakout and buy the 5th wave objective.

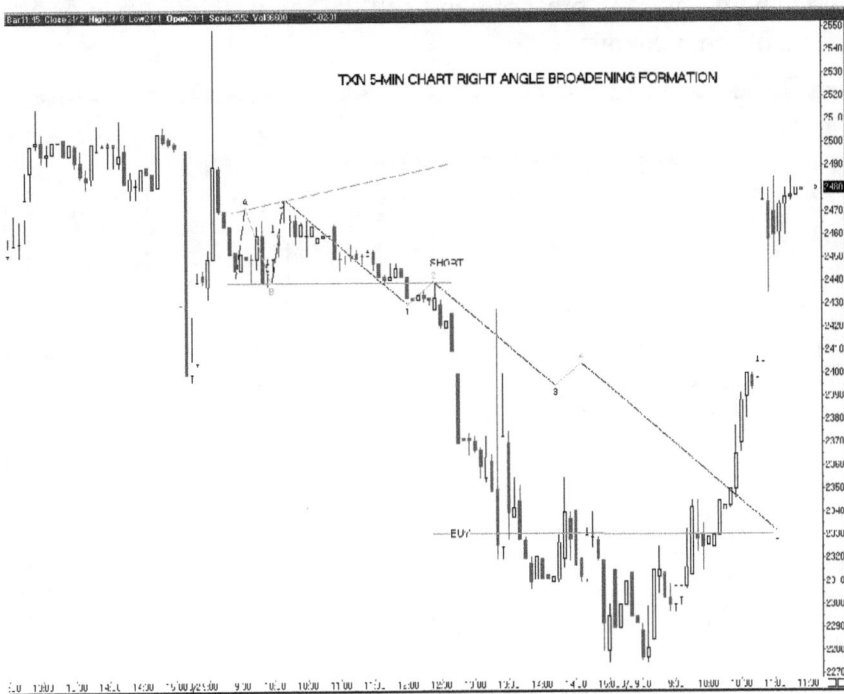

SBC 5-MIN RIGHT ANGLE DESCENDING BROADENING FORMATION

In this chart we have a Right Angle Descending broadening formation, which is bullish. Usually there is an ABC formation inside the triangle and breakout with a 5 wave or ABC formation. You should buy the breakout and sell the top of the C wave or 5th wave of the breakout.

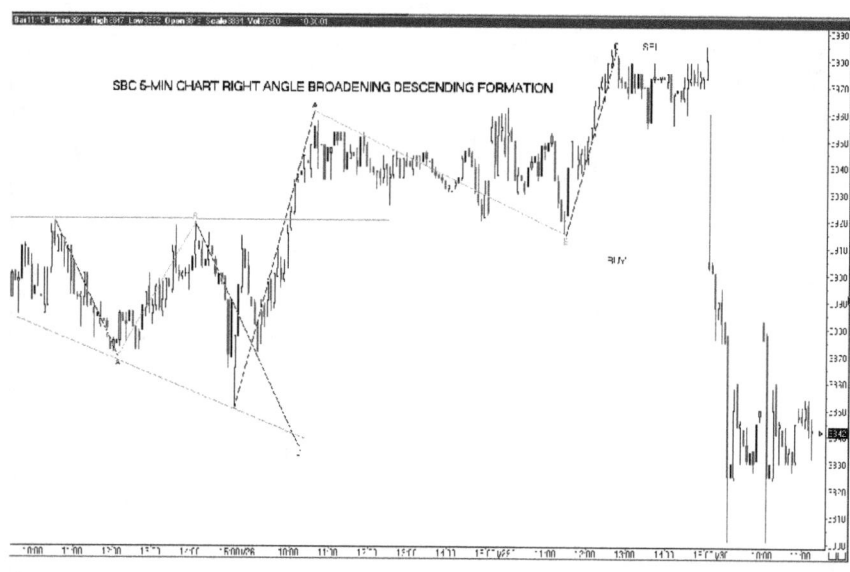

SBC 5-MIN BROADING TOP

The Broadening Top Formation is bullish. There is an ABC wave inside the formation. When the breakout occurs you should buy it and sell out at the top of wave C.

SBC 5-MIN CHART ASCENDING BROADENING WEDGE

In this example we have a Ascending Broadening Wedge which is bearish. It's usually a five-wave pattern inside the formation. After the breakout short it and take profits at the end of the C wave.

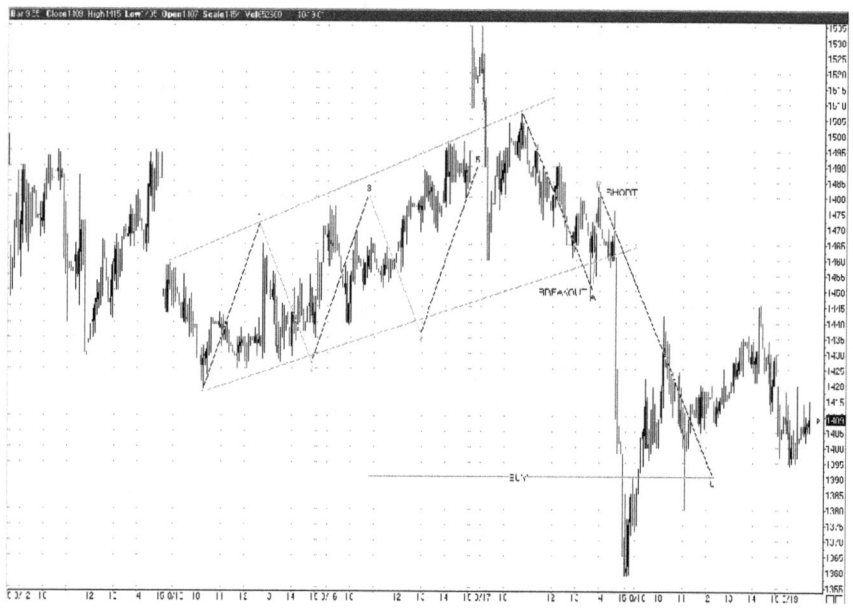

ORCL 5-MIN CHART DESCENDING BROADENING WEDGE

In the below chart we have a Descending Broadening Wedge which is bullish. It has an ABC inside pattern. The breakout can be bought on the first reaction and sold at the top of wave C.

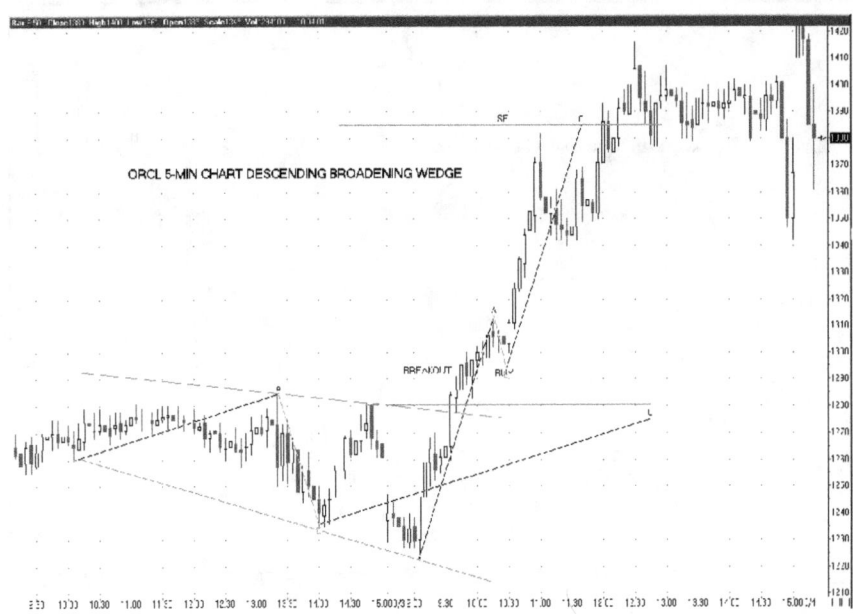

MMM 5-MIN CUP HANDLE FORMATION

The Cup Handle Formation is very powerful. It usually has an ACB inner formation with a small handle to the right of it. When it comes out it goes in a powerful five-wave formation. You can buy on the handle and hold for the end of the fifth wave.

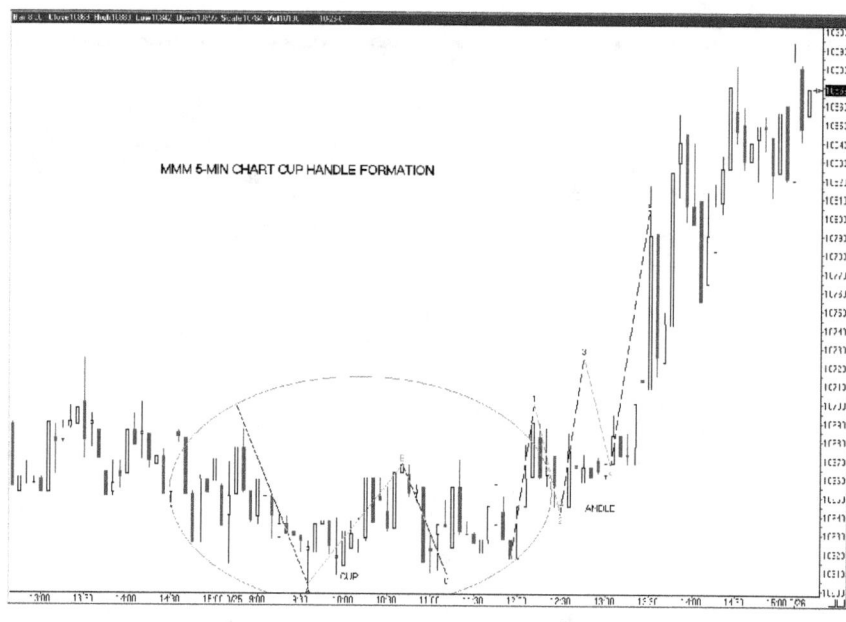

MRK 30-MIN CHART DEAD BOUNCE

When the market makes a rapid gap down in a powerful impulse it's usually a five wave down pattern. You should sell on the first bounce and take profits on the end of the fifth wave.

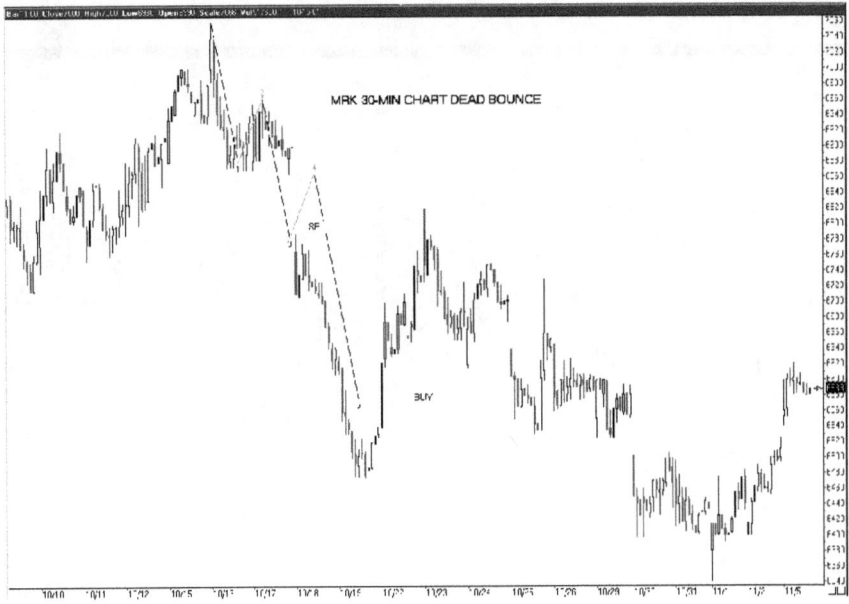

MRK 30-MIN DIAMOND TOP

At the end of a move many times you will form a Diamond Top, which is usually of 5 wave formation. When you get a breakout on the downside short it on the first reaction and take profits on the

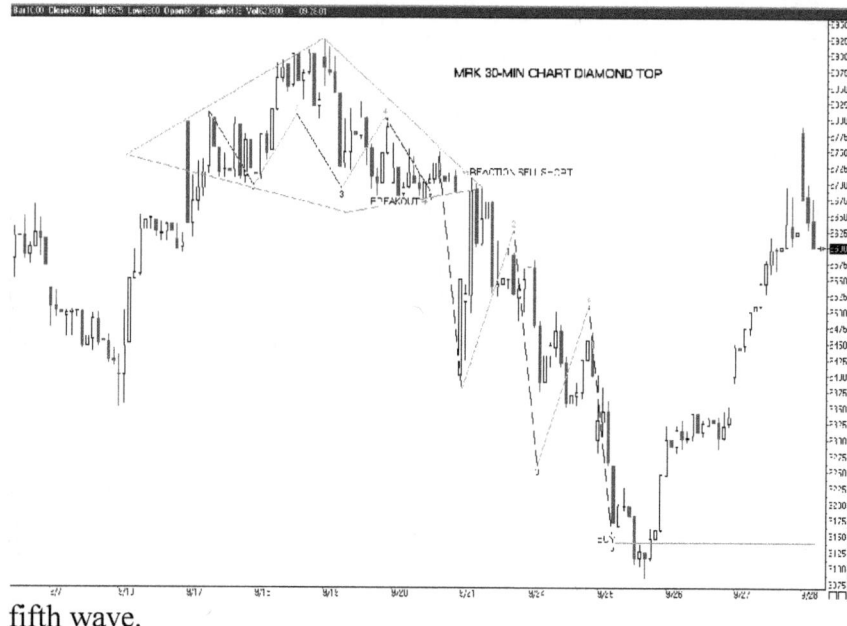

fifth wave.

MMM 30-MIN DIAMOND CONTINUATION

Many times in the middle of a move you will get a Diamond Formation, which is usually five waves. See short of the first reaction after the breakout and take profits at the end of the fifth wave.

MCD 30-MIN CHART DIAMOND BOTTOM

In the example below MCD make a diamond bottom. Buy the first

reaction and sell the fifth wave top.

SP Z1 15-MIN CHART DOUBLE BOTTOM

One of Gann's best formations was the Double Bottom. Buy on the first reaction after the breakout and sell on the fifth wave.

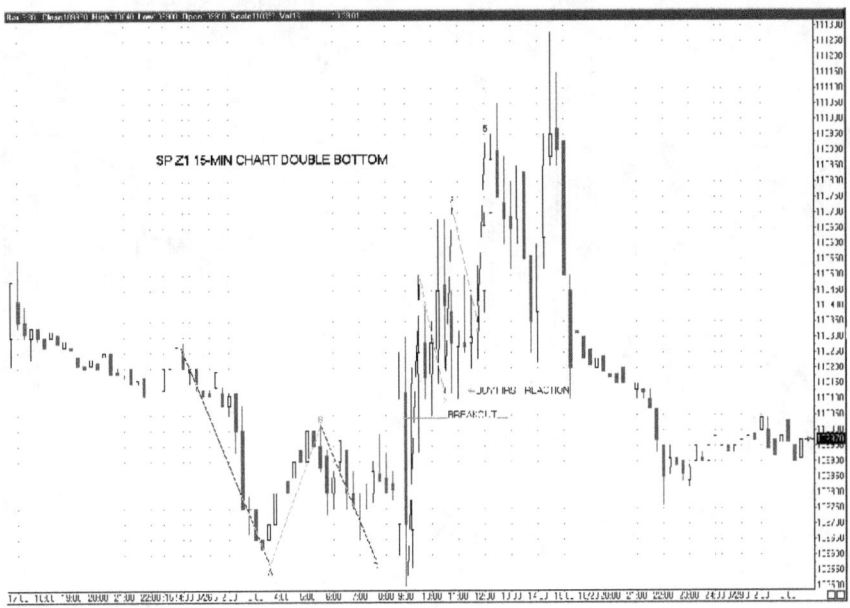

SP Z1 15-MIN CHART DOUBLE TOP

Another one of Gann's favorite signals was the double top. See on the first reaction after the breakout and take profits on the fifth wave.

EZ 15-MIN CHART BREAKAWAY GAP

In this chart you see a clear breakaway gap. You should buy on the first reaction and sell on the top of the fifth wave.

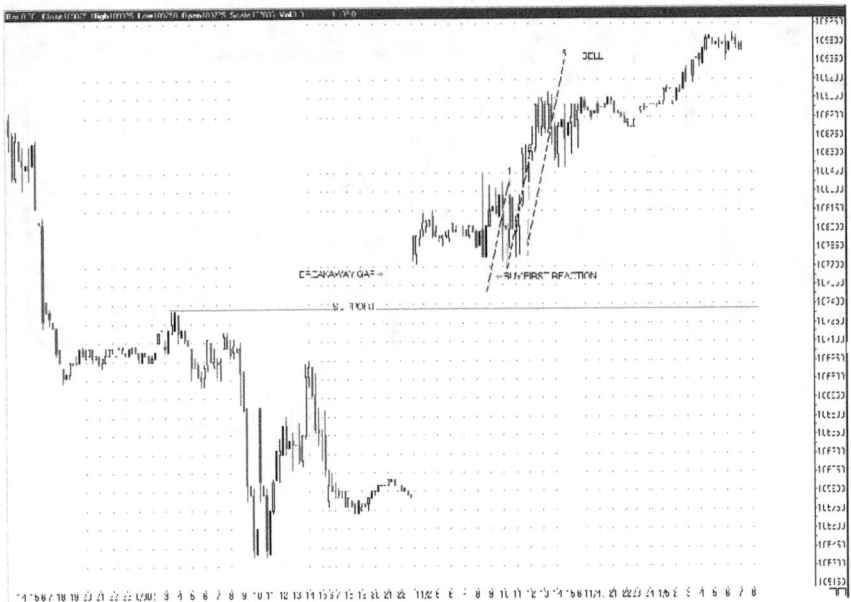

DISNEY 15-MIN CHART MIDWAY GAP

In Disney you see a Midway Gap. In this case sell on the first reaction up and take profits on the bottom of distance B.

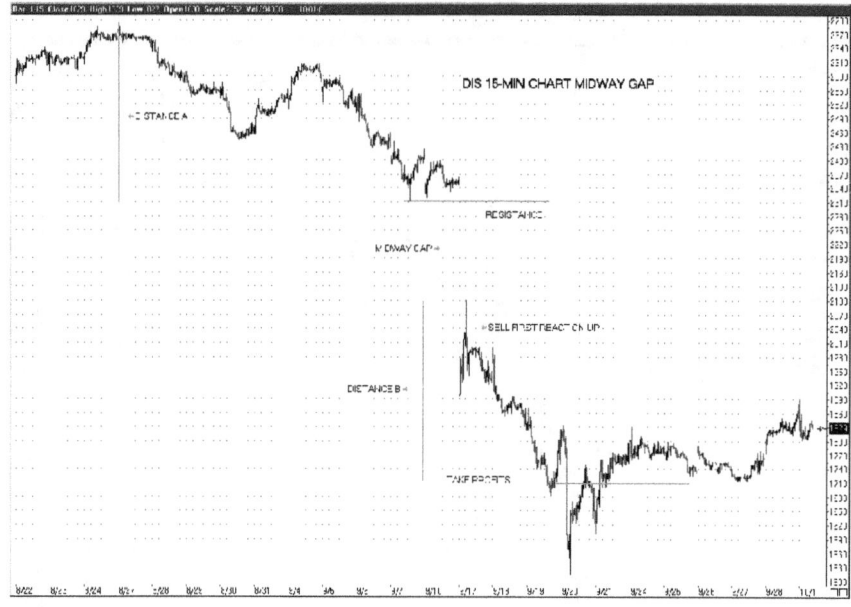

EXHAUSTION GAP

In this chart you have an exhaustion gap.

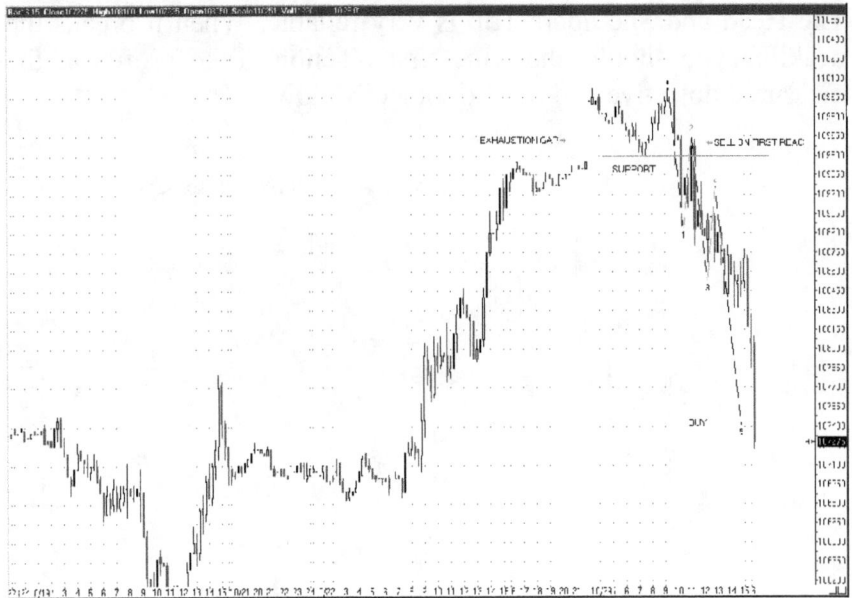

ES Z1 5-MIN CHART HEAD AND SHOULDERS TOP

The Head and Shoulders Top is very reliable. When it breaks the neckline you should short the first reaction. Take profits at the measured objective and or prior objective lows.

ES Z1 15-MIN CHART HEAD AND SHOULDERS BOTTOM

The Head and Shoulders Bottom also is extremely reliable. You buy the first reaction when the neckline is broken. Take profits up at the measured move projection.

KO 60-MIN CHART INSIDE/OUTSIDE DAYS

In many markets an inside day (that's a day that's within the prior day's range) or an outside day (that's a day that's outside of the prior days range) can signal a change of trend. It's almost amazing how many of the turns on this chart were made with inside days.

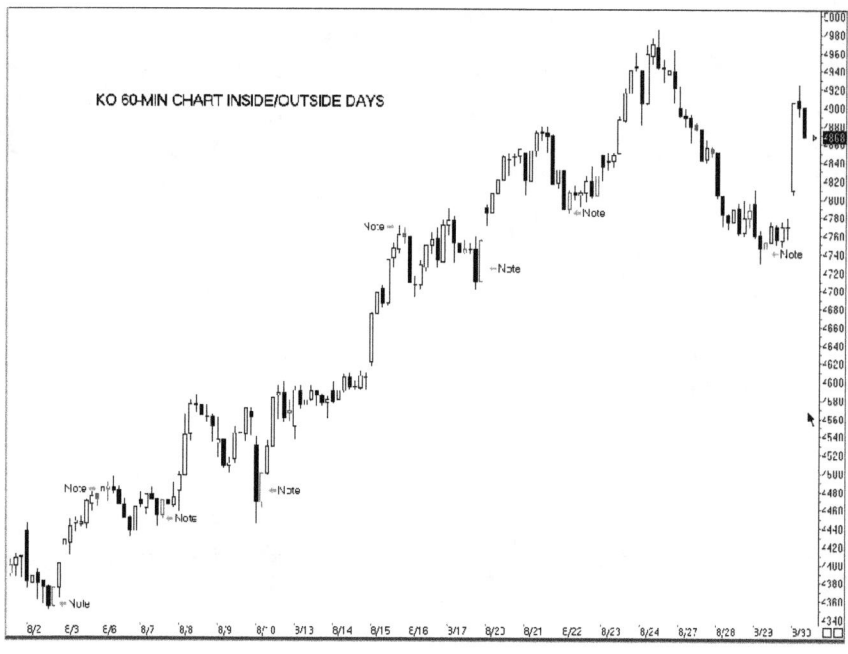

MSFT DAILY CHART ISLAND REVERSAL

Island reversals are very uncommon. When they do occur the move can be very dramatic. In this case the market took a big decline after the island occurred. You should sell in this case and put a stop on the top of the gap which would close the island reversal and nullify the signal.

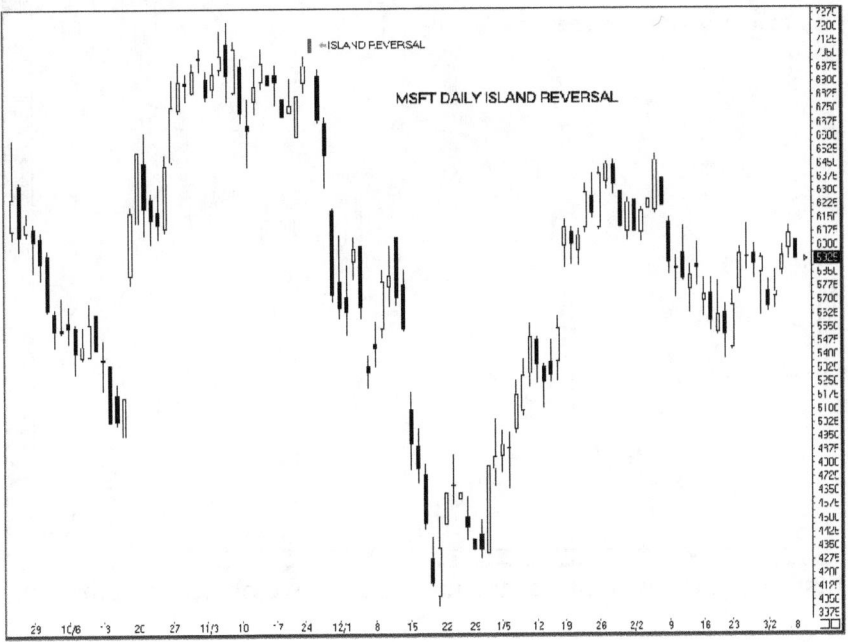

PG 30-MIN CHART RECTANGLE BOTTOM

Rectangle bottoms are very reliable. When they break out buy the

first reaction down. Sell at the measured move objective at the top.

IP 30-MIN CHART RECTANGLE TOP

The rectangle top is not found often. When it is found it gives good signals. See after the break on the first reaction up. Take profits on the first objective or the second.

DIS 5-MIN CHART RECTANGLE MIDDLE

Rectangles can also be in the middle of a move. When the formation is clearly recognized you can draw your support and resistance lines. Buy the first pullback after the breakout. Sell on the first or second objective. The objectives are measured from the height of the rectangle.

DIS 15-MIN CHART ROUNDING BOTTOM

The chart of Disney below clearly shows a rounded bottom, which happens to fit in an ellipse. Buy on the first pullback after the breakout. Sell on the objective.

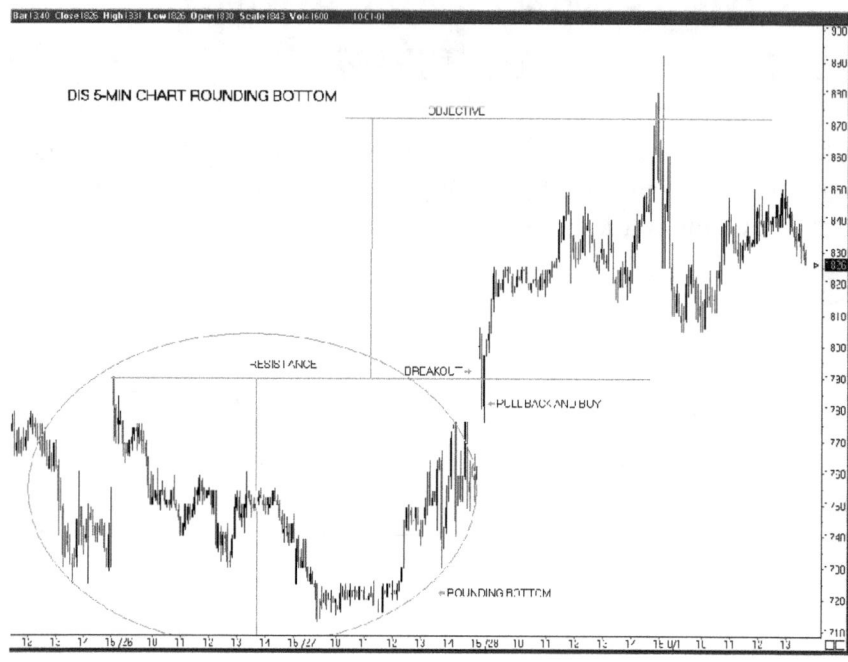

DIS 15-MIN CHART ROUNDED TOP

In this example Disney has a rounded top formed in an ellipse. When the support line is broken sell on the first reaction back up. Take profits on the objective.

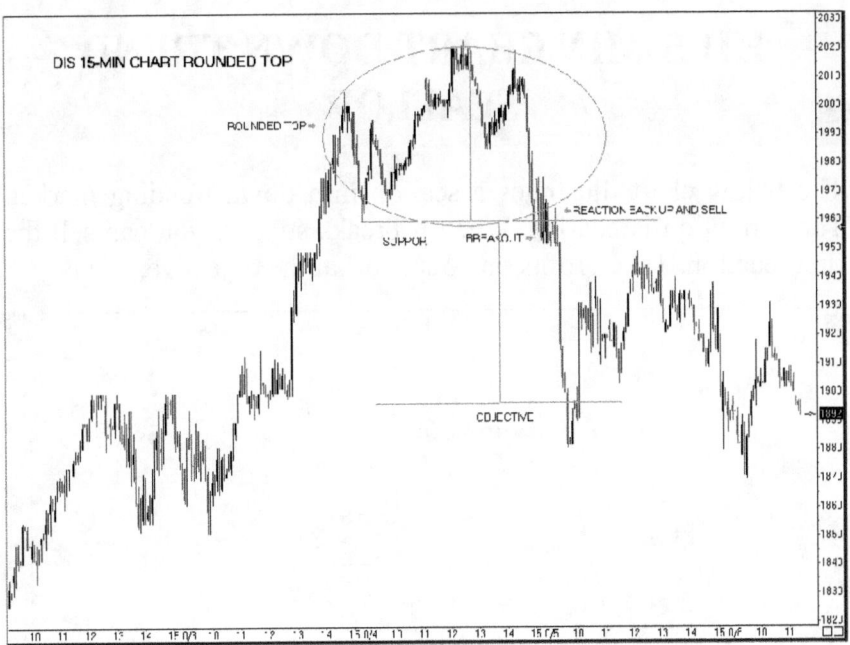

HD 5-MIN CHART DOWN TREND SCALLOP

The below chart illustrates a scallop in a down trending market. The formation is bearish. When it breaks support you can sell the first reaction. Take profits on your short at the objective.

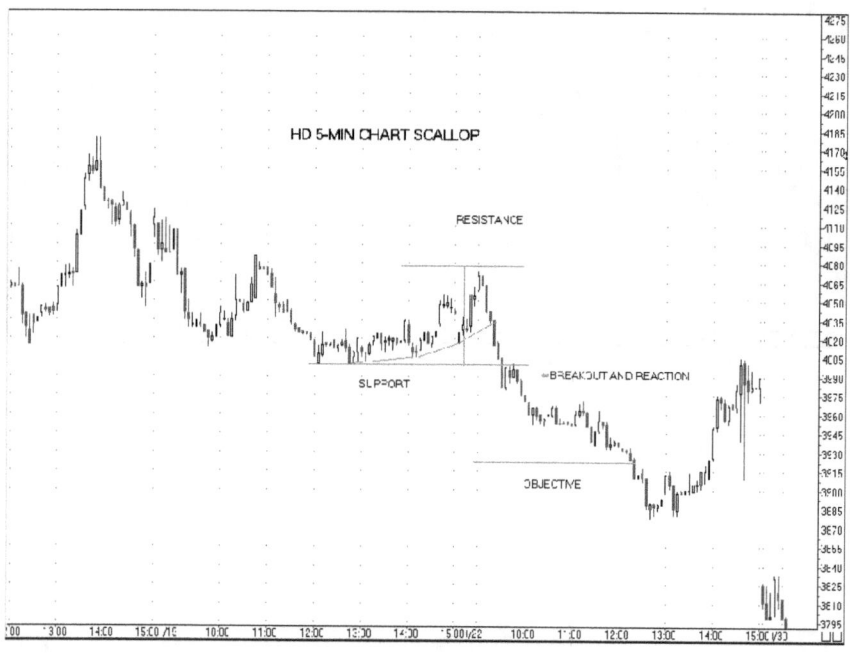

HD 5-MIN SCALLOP UPTREND

The following example shows an example of a scallop in an uptrend. After the breakout you should buy the first reaction and sell the objective when reached.

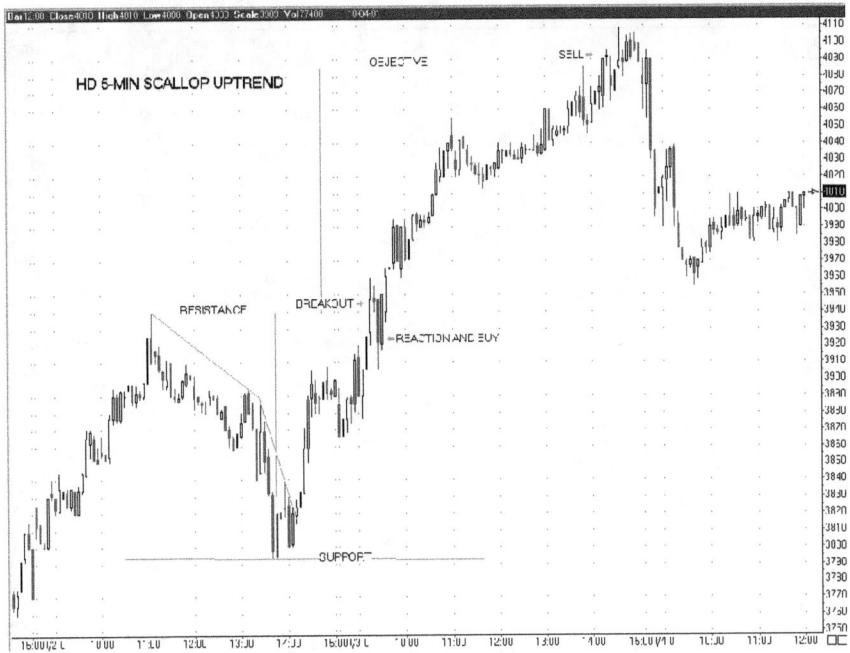

INTC 5-MIN CHART ASCENDING TRIANGLE

The below chart illustrates a descending triangle. It is a bullish

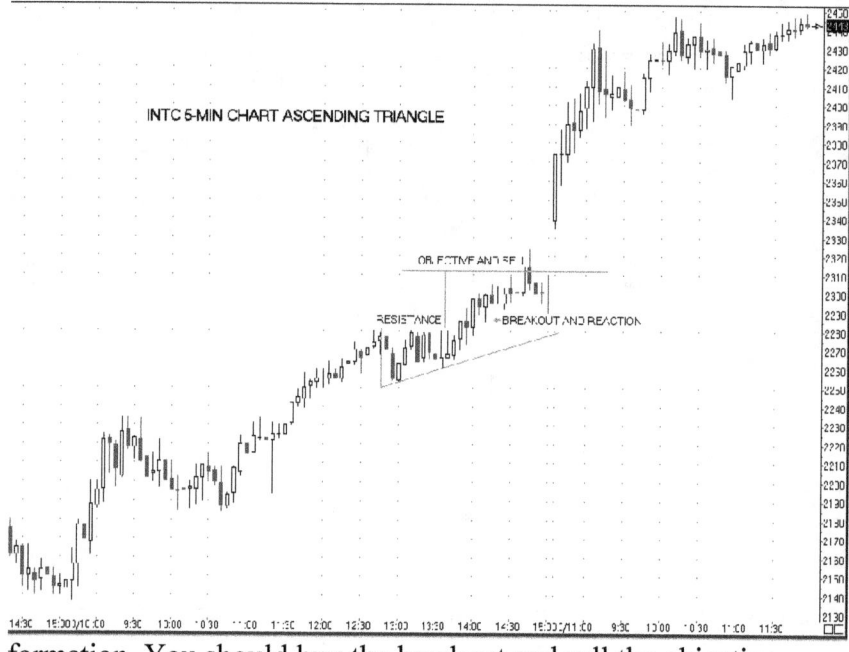

formation. You should buy the breakout and sell the objective.

GE 5-MIN CHART DESCENDING TRIANGLE

In this example a 5-Minute chart of GE is illustrated with a descending triangle. After the breakout occurs you sell the first reaction. Take profits on the objective.

DD 5-MIN CHART SYMMETRICAL TOP

Here is an example of a symmetrical top triangle. Buy the breakout and pullback and sell the objective.

EK 30-MIN CHART SYMMETRICAL BOTTOM

In this example you see a symmetrical bottom formation. After the

breakout it quickly met its objective with a one bar move.

T 15-MIN CHART TRIPLE TOP

This chart is a clear example of a 15 minute triple top. When the support is broken you can sell on the first reaction. Take profits on the objective.

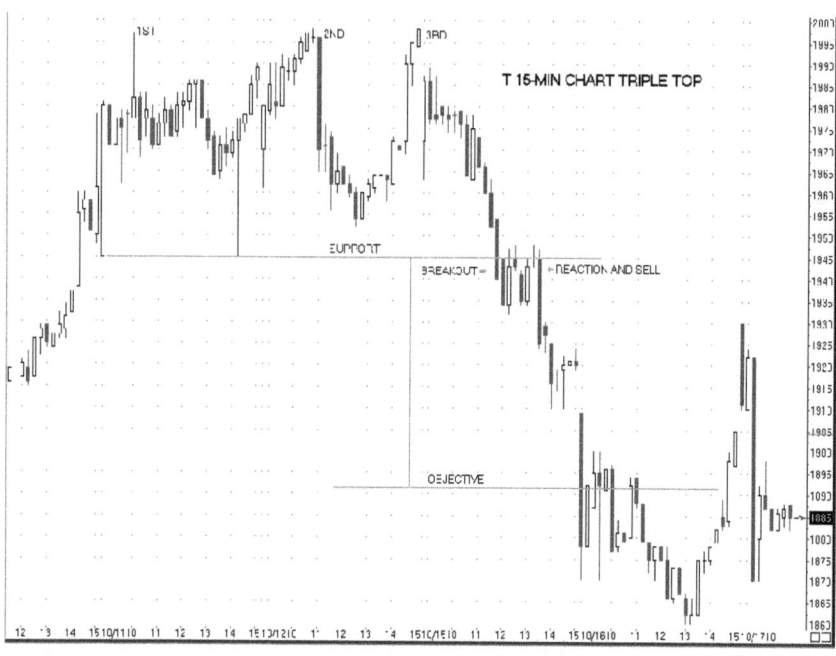

ORCL 30-MIN CHART TRIPLE BOTTOM

In this example a triple bottom clearly formed with this stock. After the breakout the stock quickly made its objective.

MRK 30-MIN CHART FALLING WEDGE

In this chart you buy the first reaction after the breakout. You sell at the top of the formation. In this case it price has only make it up 50% of its price objective.

MRK 30-MIN CHART RISING WEDGE

In this chart you see a rising wedge formation. Wait for the breakout and sell the first reaction. The price objective is the bottom of the formation, which it met in this example.

PRICE – RETRACEMENTS

The following is a chart illustrating price retracements in decimal percents The most common retracement is usually between .382 and .618.

.786 1.414

.25 .75

.382 .618

.500

1.272

1.618

1.50 2.0

PRICE – RETRACEMENTS – TWO AT THE SAME TIME

You can in many cased illustrate retracements from two points at one time. Sometimes the market will retrace to an average of the two retracements.

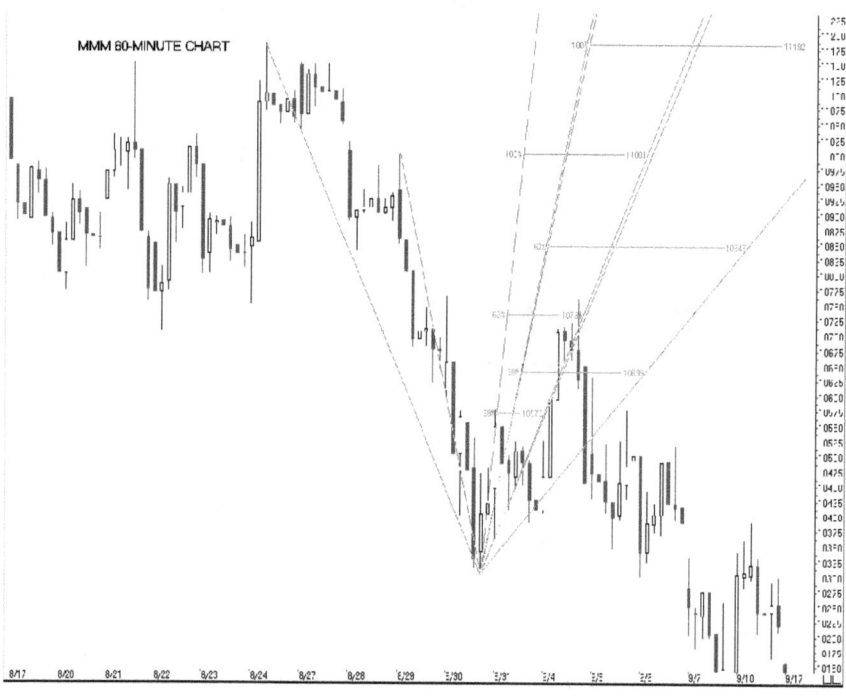

MSFT 30 MINUTE CHART

Here is another chart illustrating retracements. There again the market normally retraces between .382 and .618.

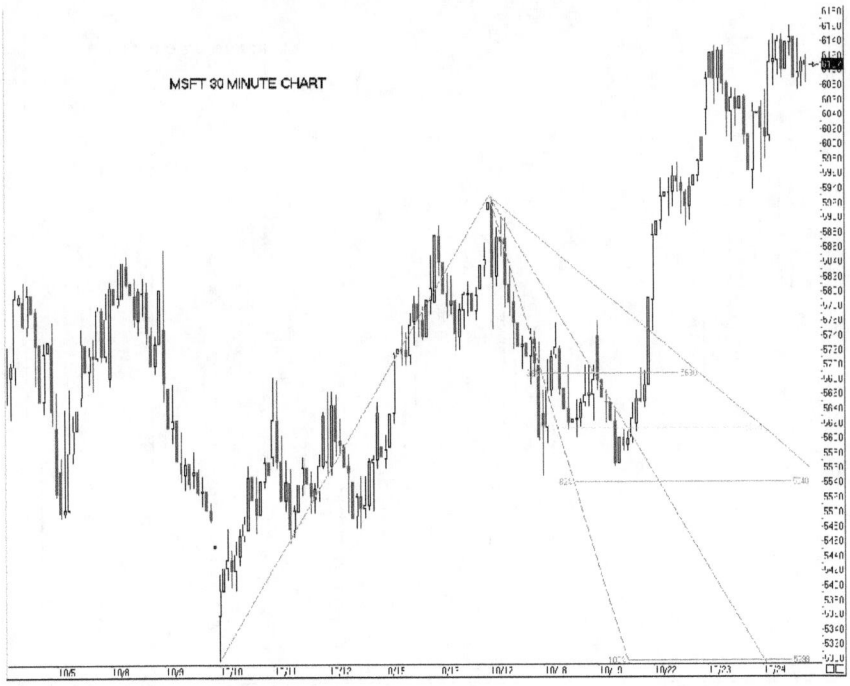

79 PERCENT RETRACEMENT

In some cased the market will retrace 79%. That is the maximum. Anything above that would be a complete change of trend.

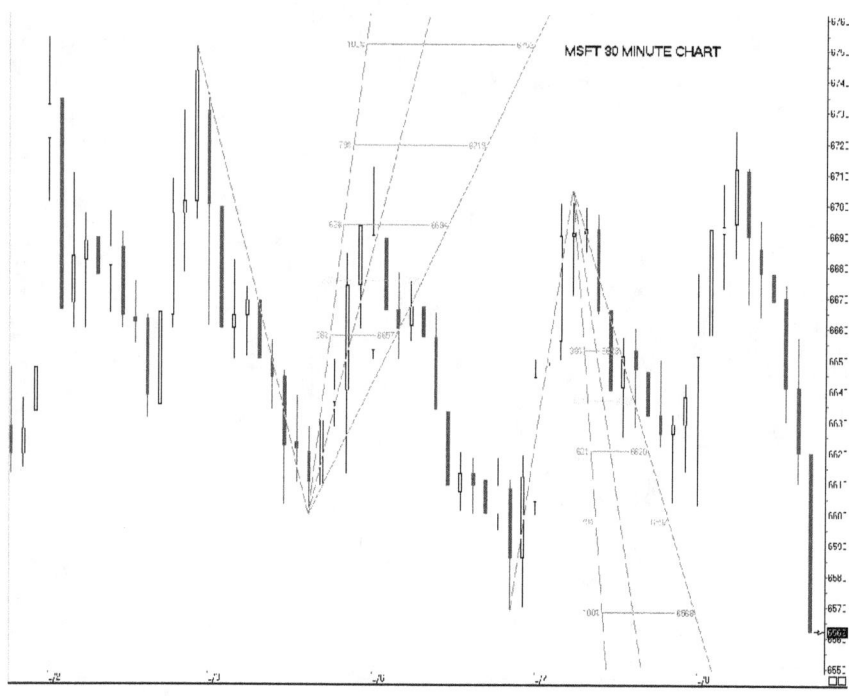

MMM 30 MINUTE 50% RETRACEMENT

The 30-minute chart is very important to traders. Here is an example of the market hitting the 50% retracement on it's first rally then falling back before trying another attempt which finally

succeeded.

MMM 30 MINUTE CHART 200% RETRACEMENT

Anything above 79% is in fact a market drive. Market drives can be 100, 150, 200 percent in one direction. Here is an illustration of a 200 retracement.

PRICE PROJECTION 1

Sometimes you can use the first price projection as a measurement for succeeding price projections. Look at this chart and the next two price projection charts.

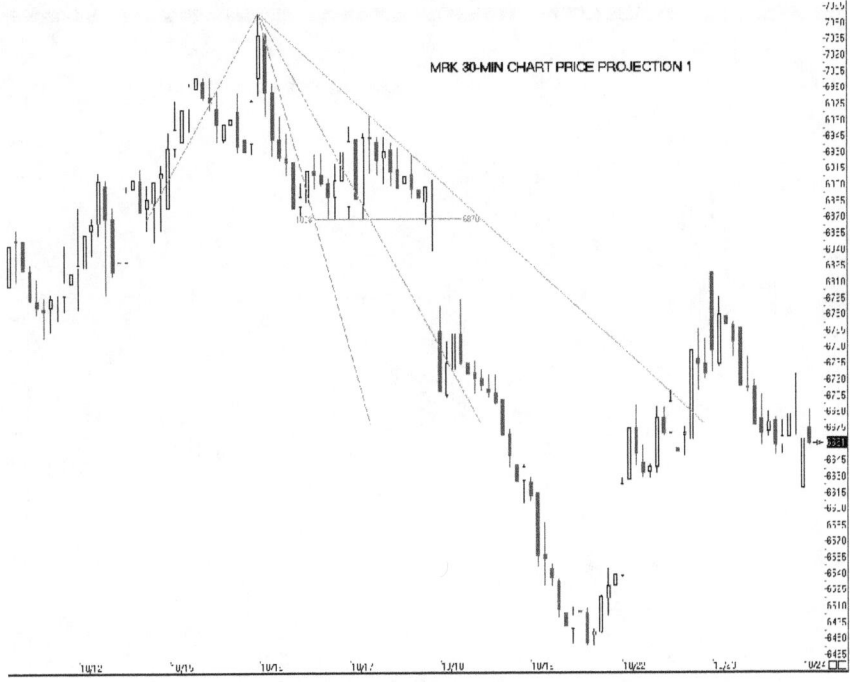

PRICE PROJECTION 2

Notice how the first price projection stops and rallied for three days before declining again.

PRICE PROJECTION 3

Notice on this projection how the price stopped at the exact point and then had a big rally.

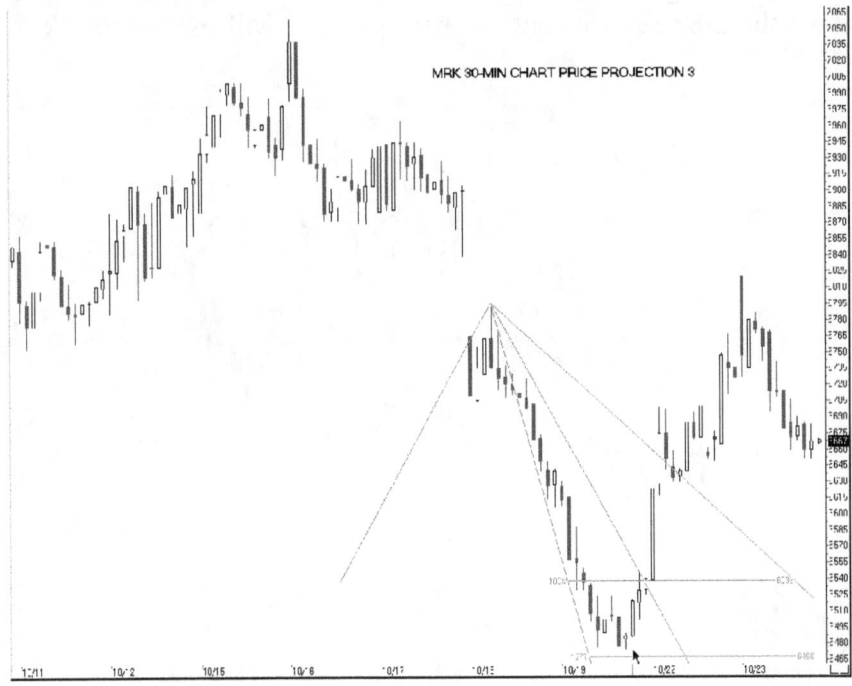

ORCL 30-MIN CHART 3 RETRACEMENTS

The following chart illustrates that most markets generally will have the .382 retracement. Sometimes they will extend to .50 to .682.

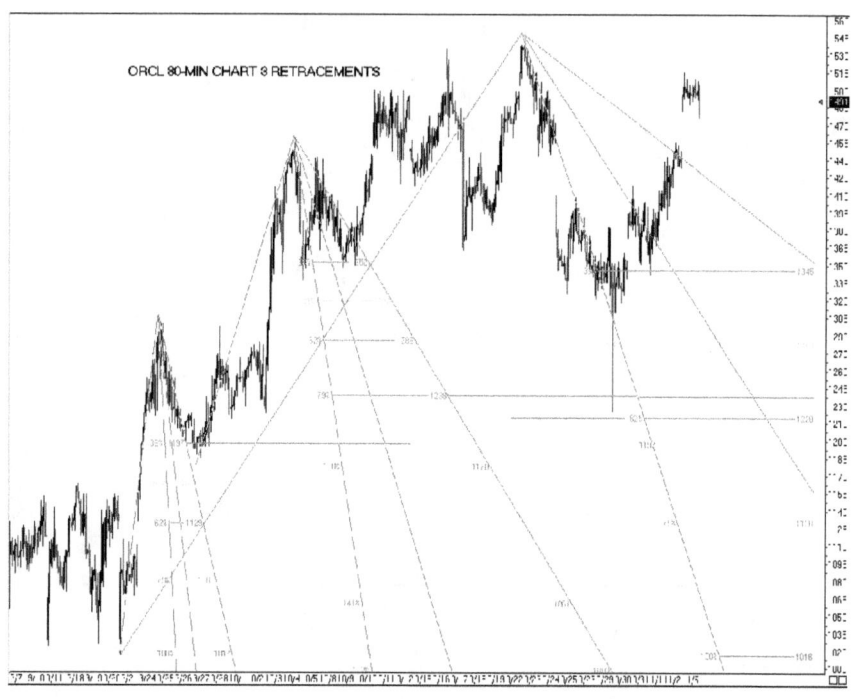

MCD 30-MIN % RETRACEMENT 1

Look at the following chart examples. Percent retracements from two bottoms can be combined together to give you objectives.

MCD 30-MIN % RETRACEMENT 2

The following shows how the second retracement hits some of the same points as the first retracement.

MRK 30-MIN TIME RETRACEMENT

Time retracements can also be used to inform you of important time points in the future.

PG 30-MIN CHART TIME ANALYSIS

Here is another example of a time retracement.

PFE 5-MIN CHART FIBONACCI CYCLES 34 AND 55

Illustrated here are the Fibonacci cycles of 34 and 55 off of bottoms and tops. The numbers of 8, 13, 21, 34, 55, 89, 144, 233 are the continuing numbers in the series, but are not illustrated here.

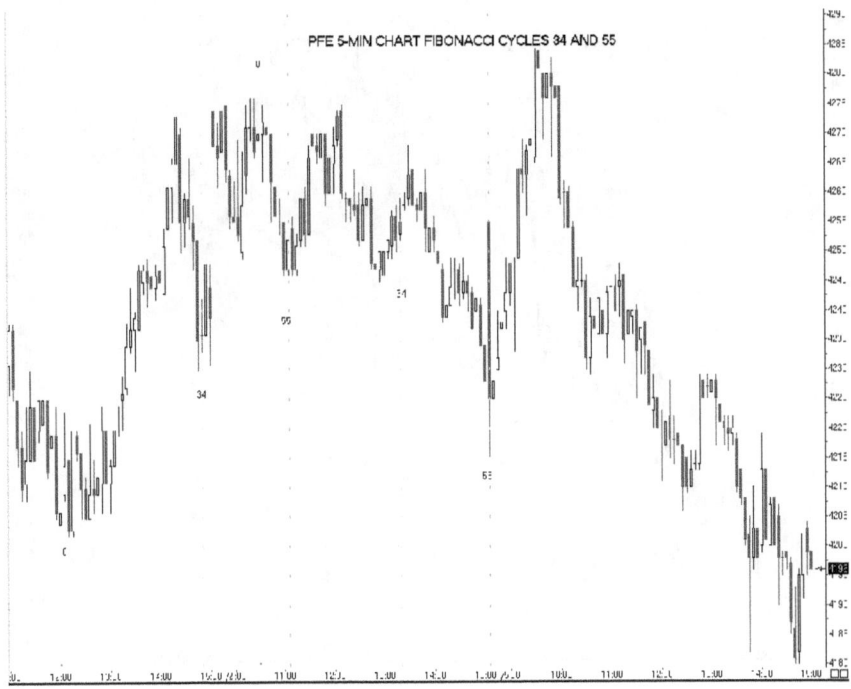

ORCL 30-MIN CHART GANN CYCLE NUMBERS

Gann Cycle Numbers of 7, 14, 21, 28, 35, 45, 90, 60, 120, 180, 270 and 360 are very important. The market often turns on these numbers. Here is an illustrated case.

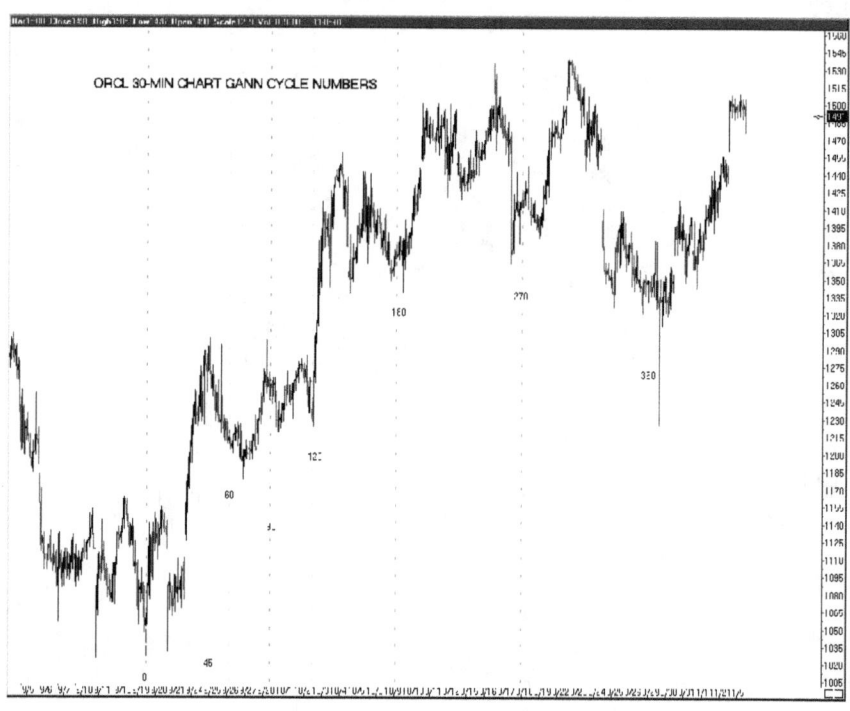

SBC 30-MIN 40 CYCLE PERIOD

Again the important cycles of the circle should be researched on every chart. That is you can divide the circle into many divisions. 40 is an important division illustrated here.

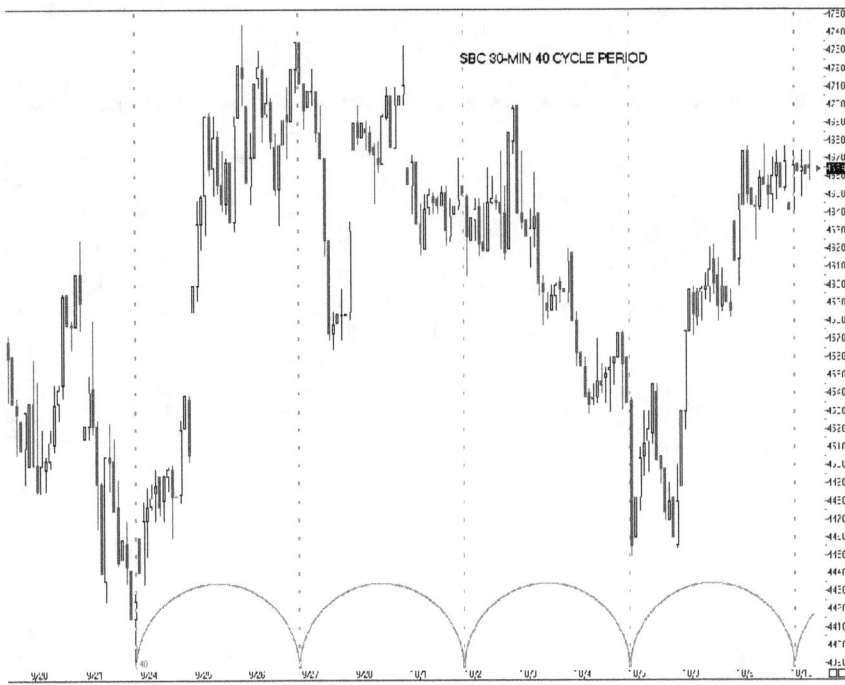

SBC 30-MIN CHART 40 CYCLE PERIOD X 3

Sometimes combination of cycles can be put together. Here we are showing how three 40-cycle periods are put together to illustrate cycles.

MSFT 60-MIN CHART WITH 5 ELLIOTT WAVES

Ensign will allow you to place three different wave patterns on the chart. You can place 3 WAVES, 4 WAVES, 5 WAVES, LARGER FIRST, LARGER LAST, LABLE A-B-C, LABLE 1-2-3. All the ratios in these waves are proportioned according to the .382 to .618 Elliott Wave ratios in both time and price.

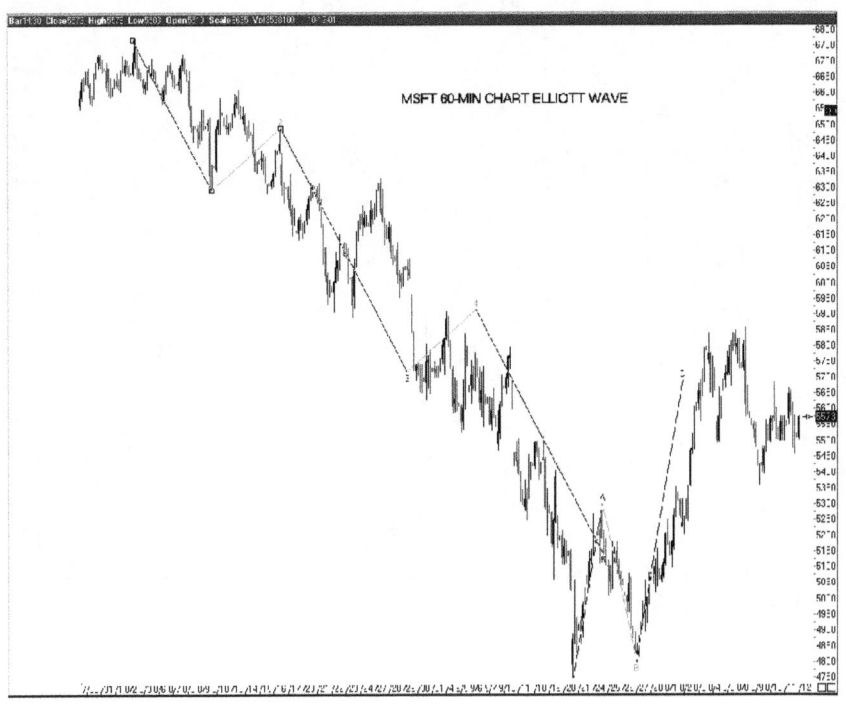

ES Z1 6—MIN CHART WITH ABC ELLIOTT WAVES

Here is an example of the ABC Swing. Look how nicely the time

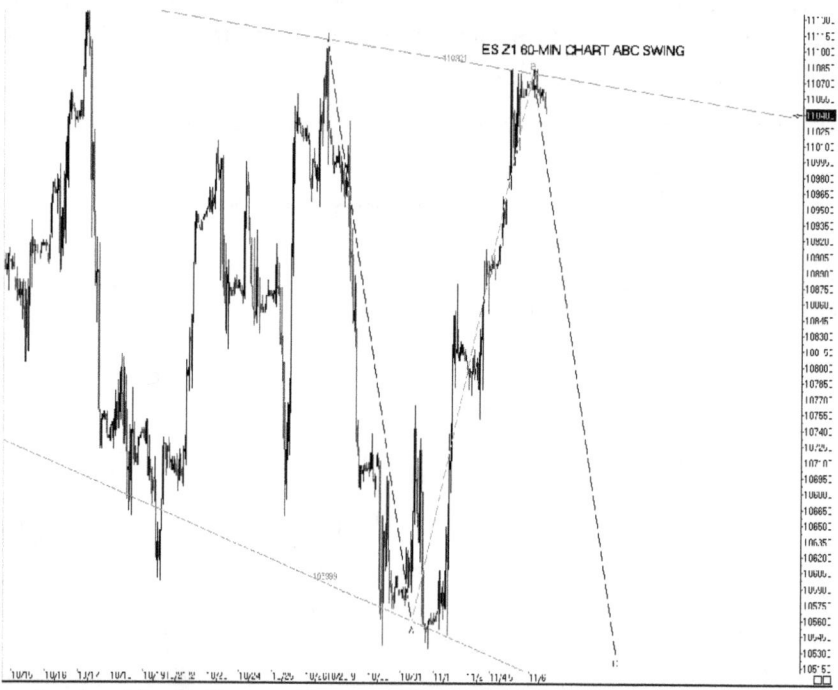

and price hits at C.

SWING CHARTS

One of Gann's favorite tools was his swing charts. The rules for trading his swing charts are very simple. You can use swing charts to give you the trend of the market in the different degrees such as daily, weekly and monthly.

Gann's trend line indicator was a 1-day swing chart. In a rising market he keep moving his trend line up until the low of the prior day was broken. When that point was broken, he moved his trend line down until the high of the prior day was broken. The principal of his 3-day swing chart is the same. Keep moving the trend line up on a rising market until the low of the last 3 days is broken. When that low is broken move the trend line down until the high of the last three days is broken.

Gann used the 3-day swing chart to tell the main trend of the market and the 1 day swing chart for the short term. The two can be combined to make a good trading system, in that when the 3-day swing chart goes long use the 1-day swing chart to enter the market. Swing charts can be based on any amount of days, weeks, months, quarters or even years. Many traders experiment and try to find the best swing chart that best fits a particular market. It is difficult to beat the combination of the 1-day and 3-day swing chart. The same combination works well on weekly, monthly and quarterly charts. For example, use a combination 1 week and a 3-week swing chart. One of Gann's favorite swing charts for the main trend was based on quarterly prices.

Swing charts can also be based on price instead of time. When the low of the prior day is broken by say 2 cents in corn the trend line turns down. The trend line stays down until the market reverses up over the prior days high by 2 cents.

To increase the effectiveness of swing charts you can also use both time and price in the formula. By that, I mean that if on a 3 day swing chart the price declines below the prior day's low it must also decline a certain amount of cents also to confirm the down turn. For example in Corn the price must break the prior 3-day's low and also break the low by 2 cents to confirm the change of trend. If doesn't break both the time and price point, then the trend line indicator remains up.

Swing charts are effective for seeing a change of price trend both on the short term and the main trend. The swing chart is a good place for you to know where to place stops. Stops can be placed below or above the last important swing points.

Swing charts are excellent for entering the market after a correction has occurred. For example, when a main uptrend has turned down, use the 1 day uptrend chart to enter the market when the prior days low is broken by 2 cents.

Swing charts should be watched very carefully with the concept of overbalancing prior time and price points. For example, if in the last three corrections in a major uptrend, corn retraced no more than 10 days and 20 cents, do not consider that the main trend turning down until the current correction exceeds the 10 days and 20 cents of the last biggest correction.

Time and price swing charts have many problems. They often give bad signals to the trader. Using past historical data our research has found that using price correction is not as effective as time calculation. Time, as Gann said is the most important factor. Percentage retracements of the last swing has proven to be more effective than price retracements. In a bull market the percentage retracements should be less and less as you go up. If the percentage retracements start to get bigger, then it is an indication that the trend is changing. Once a prior swing percentage retracement is exceeded there is a loss of momentum and it is possible that the market is topping.

Another way to check the market's strength is to do a check of the markets price and time swings in the direction of the main trend of the market. When they are less than the prior advancements the market is losing momentum.

To check the strength of the market's strength, you can also figure the market's percentage swing of the last two moves. When this percentage starts declining, there is a possible change of trend coming.

Many times when a swing chart is broken, it also gives another indication of a change of trend, such as a reversal day. This was one of Gann's favorite signals. There are three basic reversal days: A gap up and reverse day, a hook reversal and a key reversal. So you can monitor both retracements and advances for their swing properties we have programmed a spread sheet module for this purpose.

With this spread sheet template you can put in the high and low of swings as the market is moving up. The spread sheet will automatically calculate the points of the reaction. If the points come up close to a Gann number then more importance is put on it. The spread sheet also calculates the % retracement for each swing.

When the market advances to a new high, the spread sheet will calculate the points move and the percentage of the move. This gives you an indication of the strength of the market. From this you can tell the strength of the market. This tells you that momentum is increasing or declining.

A swing chart can be set up based on the information coming from our spread sheet module. For example, if the price breaks under the prior 3 day low by 2 cents, if the market exceeds a 3 day reaction, if the market reacts more than 20% of the last move up, then start moving the trend line down.

This spread sheet can also be used effectively to spot when there is an overbalance of time, price and percent. When all three confirm an overbalance of time, price and percentage there is a major change of direction.

DOUBLE AND TRIPLE TOPS AND BOTTOMS

One of Gann's most important rules was to sell double and triple tops with a stop above the market and buy double bottoms and triple tops with a stop below the market. The bigger the amount of time involved in the double or triple top, the more important the resultant move will be. The breakout of a weekly double or triple top is more important than the breakout of a daily double or triple top. The breakout of a monthly double or triple top is more important than a weekly breakout.

In our research we have found that double and triple bottoms are more common than double or triple tops. That is because it is easier to build a base at a bottom than at a top. Tops are usually formed under high volume with many traders in the market and volume is much higher. Bottoms are usually formed with light volume and few traders.

With a double or triple bottom, rising bottoms are stronger than just flat bottoms. With rising bottoms, the market is showing that there is not enough weakness for the second or third bottom to get down to the bottom. Therefore the market is much stronger.

Buying the breakouts of a double or triple tops or selling breakdowns of double and triple bottoms is usually a very safe play as you are going with the direction and momentum of the market.

There is a method that works very well with Gann double and triple tops and bottoms. The method uses a displaced moving average. This method actually defines a double or triple top or bottom. It's necessary to do back testing of prior tops and bottoms of the same commodity or stock to get the best working combination of moving average and displacement unit. What works in the past with a market, will usually work with a present market.

When the market makes a fourth attempt that results in a failure it will usually result to a fast move the other direction. Watch the fourth attempt closely. When the market brakes below the moving average three times and the closing low point and then reverses and goes through the 4th top reverse and go the direction of the market.

Know where you are in the pattern of the market. A triple bottom is much more important in the beginning phase of a major 5 wave move up. It must know the Elliott wave patterns of the market. Many markets have a particular pattern of their own that develops at important tops and bottoms.

If a breakout occurs from a double or triple bottom, it is important that any reactions must not be over three weeks. If this occurs watch the fourth week closely for the direction of the market. If that fourth week in a major uptrend has a lower high and then falls under the third week's low the uptrend is probably over.

If the market makes three tops and then breaks down and then makes a fourth and fifth attempt, which are lower lows, then the market is very weak and should break sharply. These tops must be defined by the displaced moving average method. If the market makes three bottoms and then breaks up and then makes a fourth and fifth bottom, which

are higher then the market is very strong. These bottoms also must be defined by the displaced moving average.

This displaced moving average method of defining double and triple tops and bottoms gets you in the market safer than if you took your trade at the exact double or triple tops or bottoms.

VOLUME AND OPEN INTEREST

Gann felt that volume and open interest was very important to indicate market direction. This chapter will explain how to use these tools for indications of direction of trend. Volume is what drives the market. This indicates if there is increasing demand for the supply in the market. Look closely at the trend of the volume. This will help you determine if trend of the market will continue.

Volume is the number of contracts that traded during the day. It represents either the purchases or sales, but not both. The more activity on the floor the more volume there is. This can increase due to day trading or overnight trading.

If volume does not increase or decrease then speculators feel the market will remain steady. Volume usually remains steady in consolidation areas, usually at low price levels. If price moves out of a consolidation area with increased volume, then there is a good chance that the price move will be the beginning of a good move. If price moves out of a consolidation area and volume does not increase, then there is a good chance that it is a false breakout and the price will fall back into the consolidation area.

If prices start to fall out of a consolidation area with increased volume it is significant. If prices start to rise out of a consolidation area with increased volume then it is significant. If when price falls the volume starts to fall, then the market may be ready for a turn back up.

If the volume increases when price falls back to a base, it means that traders are buying it as they think it is a bargain. If volume increase when prices run up to a resistance area, it means traders are unloading it thinking price is too high.

Volume also increases when the market runs into stops. The floor traders often times run the market into these areas when they can. If the market has run up into stops and does not continue, then these is a good chance prices will fall back as it just got the weak shorts who had to put in close stops.

For a big trend to continue, the volume must continue to rise. Watch the volume closely as it will give you the clue to the market direction. Without increasing volume, prices will not continue to increase.

After a long advance in prices many times the volume increases dramatically because small speculators are jumping into the market near the top thinking that prices will continue up forever.

After a long decline in the market many times volume will dramatically increase because the public who have been long the market and loosing lots of money are finally giving up and throwing in the towel. In this case the market will soon reverse as professional traders are buying the contracts from the small speculators.

When prices break out of a consolidation area and make their first advance and then decline, if the volume runs up and then declines it is bullish.

When prices break down out of a consolidation area and makes their first decline and then makes the first correction back up, if it decline is on heavy volume and the retracement back up is on declining volume then this is a good indication for a good move down.

Open interest is when there is a new buyer of a contract and a new seller. These two parties cross. The buyer buys and the seller sells making a complete transaction. The open interest then increases by 1 contract.

When prices increase with rising volume and open interest increases this is a further indication that the market will rise. Having all three rise is very bullish.

If prices are rising, with rising volume and decreasing open interest, then it is a good indication that there is short covering in the market. These traders are liquidating their contracts to get out of the market. When this happens the market will not trend much further.

If prices are stable and open interest is rising there is a good indication that positions are being accumulated. This is especially true if you are in a level of support such as wave 2 or 4 in the Elliott wave pattern.

If prices are stable and open interest is stable, there is no indication of any change of trend. Look for the market to break out of a consolidation range with rising open interest and volume to change this stable condition of the market.

If prices are stable and open interest is falling then there is a good indication that the market is losing interest and the public is going elsewhere.

GANN CHANNELS

Gann placed the geometric angles on important tops, bottoms to indicate the trend of the market. These geometric angles accurately measure space, time, volume and price. The angles to draw on these tops and bottoms are the 1x8, 1x4, 1x3, 1x2, 3x4, 2/3, 1x1, 4x3, 3x2, 2x1, 3x1, 4x1 and 8x1. These angles determine all important tops and bottoms. These angles drawn on a chart divide time and price into proportionate parts.

To determine the angle you should draw you should look at the price it is moving off of. If the price is, for example, at a bottom of 72, then the market will move up 72 hours, days, weeks or months. You may just want to use the best angle that fits initial price move best.

What I mean by one square up are the squares that are on the Gann overlays. For example the squares on the 144 overlay are 144/8 = 18 or multiples thereof. That is they are 2.25, 4.5, 9, 18, 36, 72. The square of 120/8 = 15 or multiples thereof. That is they are 7.5, 15, 30, 60. The square of 90/8 = 11.25. Those multiples are 5.625, 11.25, 22.50, 45, 90. The square of 52/8 = 6.5. Multiples are 13, 23, and 46. You must know the square overlay that the market is working in. Once the height of the channel is determined, prices will usually remain in the channel height until the market accelerates or direction the market changes trend. Where an angle starts off you can draw a square, which is the same measurement high and wide. Timing and price projection should be based on this square.

Using a fast MACD and a slow stochastic on your charts you can determine where to buy the bottom of 2(C) and 4(C). In most cases the MACD will get above the center point, putting the market in a strong position and the stochastic will drop down to the 20% line and give a double bottom with divergence. In buying watch the stochastic and the bars on the chart. When the market moves up and makes a new daily high after the turn up of stochastic, you should buy the market. It is also possible to use the stochastic to take profits when price gets to the top of the channel and divergence is occurring. Remember never go short the market based on stochastics in an uptrend as the market can continue to advance.

After the 5th wave top is made and MACD gets under the center point, you can sell the first stochastic high B wave and go short the market. The procedure is just the reverse of buying the bottom. Watch the down wave C very carefully to determine in this is in fact a down wave beginning to start or just and ABC and resumption of the main trend up again.

CAPITAL REQUIRED

It is very important that you understand the amount of capital required to trade the markets. You want to have the ability to continue to trade the markets without being wiped out. Most traders have no capital trading plan, use fear and greed to trade by, and over trade. It's no wonder that 90% of commodity traders lose. Those 10 % that do make money, of course, are the ones that have learned how to trade. They make all the money that the others lose. If you make a plan of capital preservation, you will always have the necessary capital to trade with, even if you have the expected losses in the markets. If you put all your capital at risk in the markets on a couple trades, like so many traders do, then you will surely lose it all and be out of the game. "Preservation of capital" is your first rule to apply with all your trades.

On the Chicago Board of Trade, the grains trade in units of 5000 bushels. When wheat is trading where it is now at $3.50 - $3.75 per bushel, you need 20% of the value of the total contract to safely trade the market, though the exchanges charge only 5% margin. If you fully leverage your position on the 5% margin, you will be scared out of the markets with fear and greed and will surely lose, so use the 20% margin rule to safeguard your capital. If wheat is selling at $3.75, you would multiply this amount times 5000 bushels to get $18,750 as the total value of the contract. 20% of the contract value is $3750. Therefore to trade a 5000 bushel contract of wheat at $3.75, you should have $3750 of capital. The exchange margin on a contract of wheat at that level is about $1000 or 5%. You therefore have an excess of $2750 over the initial margin required. Divide the $2750 by 10 giving you a potential of 10 trades possible with a maximum loss of $275 each before you're out of the game. Your average risk should never be more than 10% of the excess capital above the initial margin rate of the contract. You should have enough money to trade the market 10 times, and have ten straight losses, before you would be wiped out. This should never happen, if you have a trading plan and trade according to the rules of successful trading, which you will learn in this course. It's very rare that you would even have three consecutive losses, and even if you did, then the next trade could make you 10% on your money giving you a large gain over your small losses. Your capital for trading commodity markets should be at least 20% of the total contract value. You should never risk more than 10% of your excess margin money on any one trade, so you can trade at least 10 times before you are out of the game. If the market is in a major up trend, as the market gets higher, you will need more capital to trade. If wheat rises to $4.50 per bushel, you will need $4500 to trade each contract and you would never risk more than 10% of your excess margin capital on each trade, so you could have 10 losing trades before you were out of the market.

In the stock market, the capital requirement rules are different. If you buy stocks, you have two choices, either put up the full purchase price of the stock or put the stock on margin and put up 50% of the value of the stock and pay interest on the other 50% usually at 1% above broker call rate. In either case, you still must follow the rules of capital preservation. Never risk more than 10% of your trading capital above the initial margin required on any one trade. If you purchase 100 shares of a stock at $50.00 per share the total amount of the transaction is $5000. I am not taking into account commission for this example, but for your own trading you also need to take into account commission costs. If you purchase this on margin, you would have to put up 50% or $2500. You should have at least 50% of the total value of the stock above the initial margin. Divide this 50% into 10 equal parts to figure out what amount each stop should be. You can vary this percent, but it must be based on how active the stock is. If you use the same rule that is used in commodities, you would not risk more than 10% of the excess margin on any one trade. Therefore in this case, 50% of the total value of the stock is $2500 and that divided into 10 equal parts is $250 maximum loss per trade to stay in the game.

Margin for trading a contract of wheat

3.75 per bushel X 5000 bushels

$1850 X 20%

= $3750 necessary capital - $1000 initial capital

= $2750 excess capital divided by 10

In day-trading the margins are different for commodities. You are only required to put up 50% of the normal margin required. You still should follow the above rules as the risk is still there. To day-trade stocks its now a necessity to have an account of $25,000 or over to avoid exchange clearing problems. This was a new rule enacted last year to stem the excessive day-trading that was being done by the public.

Generally it is much easier to day-trade commodities. The margins are less and the mechanics are easier. For example in commodities if you buy a contact of corn as a day-trade you put up 50% margin. If you short a contract you again have to only put up 50% margin. It's very simple. In stocks if you buy and sell excessively during the day you are required to have an account of $25,000. If you short you must also borrow the stock from another margin account. The firm you are trading with must give you permission to short once they have secured the shares from another customer on margin. In theory, it rarely happens, if the other party sells their stock and you have it short, you will get a call that you must cover your short and give the stock back. In addition, if you are short a stock on a dividend day you must pay the dividend to the shareholder of record. Another very serious problem with shorting stocks is that if you are short and a company buys out the stock you might have a hard time replacing the stock and get caught in a financial squeeze.

TYPES OF ORDERS

You need to have a consistent plan for entering and exiting the market. There are different types of orders for entering the market. Most of the exchanges will accept any of the types of orders. The orders you place will be designed for two purposes. One to enter into a new position and to exit or stop out of your current position with a stop loss. The following are the types of orders you can use:

Market Order

When you use this type of order, you want the floor broker to fill your order immediately without any delay in time. It is used by traders who want to enter or exit the market as fast as they can without any regard to price. In most cases when this type of order is used you will lose a few points on the filled of the order by a floor scalper.

Or Better Orders

With this type of order, you want the floor broker to fill you at the price you put on the order or even better than you put. If this is an order to buy it is put above the market and if market price drops to your price or lower your order will be filled. You will rarely find that you get a better fill than you put as your price on the order. Sell or better orders are placed below the price put on the order. When the price rises and hits or goes high than the price put on the order it is filled. Again, rarely is the ordered filled at a price better than the one put on the order.

Some successful traders use this type of order to enter a trade based on a timing point. If they are not filled within a specified amount of time they change the order to market.

Market if Touched Orders

A market-if-touched sell order is placed below the indicated price on the order. If and when prices go up and hit that price, it is filled at the market. Therefore it is possible that the fill could be below the price put on the ticket. In the case of market-if-touched buy orders if the market falls down and hits the price on the order it is filled at the market price. If order is good to use if you have calculated the exact price the market should go to and you want out if it hits that price.

Market On Close Orders

This type of order is used if you want out at the market in the last closing minutes of the day. Your order becomes a market order and fills at any price at the close of the day. This type of order is used by day-traders who want out on the close of the day at any cost. Also many traders enter the market based of how it looks like it is going to close. In this situation market-on-close orders do the job. Market-on-close orders can also be a limit order. The price must not exceed the limit price on the order or it doesn't fill.

One Cancels the Other Order

With this type of order you can put an order in at a certain price and another order in a price. If one of the orders is filled the other order is cancelled.

Stops

Gann constantly said, always put a protective stop loss in the market as the market could turn against you anytime. Forecasting the market is all probabilities and therefore you need protection, just in case the market doesn't cooperate with you. This protection is necessary to preserve your capital. Gann felt that the stop should be placed as soon as your entered your buy order.

Stops can be placed on the basis of money using the rule of dividing your risk capital into 10 equal parts so no more than 10% is ever exposed to the market. This was explained in an earlier chapter.

Stops can be placed below the last swing bottom in the market. This swing bottom should be placed on the basis of time, price and percentage retracement swing charts. By using stops you will in many cases remain in the market for the entire market move.

Time Stops

Many traders use a time stop. The exchanges won't accept them, but they can save a lot of money. With this type of stop, if the market does not give you a profit within a certain time period, for example 3 days, you simply exit the position.

MAKING IT WORK

If you want to be successful, follow all the rules in this course. Everything that you read and learn in this course must be proved to yourself. Do not jump in and start trading until you are ready to trade. All the trading techniques must be programmed into your mind so you don't even think about them anymore. You must feel completely at ease and have no fear toward trading whatsoever. You must be ready to enter into the market when the public is being scared out. You must not enter into the market when the public feels that nothing can go wrong. 90% of the public looses money in the market.

The first thing you must do is get files of long term daily data that go back long enough to prove that Gann rules do work. Go back using the data and prove all rules that you have learned. You can use long term paper charts for this, or you can use long-term computer files for this. If you are using computer files, make sure you have the equipment that makes these files look like long term paper charts on your computer screen. That is, you should have a program like Ensign that can display charts properly.

The Excel spread sheet program is a necessity for trading successfully. Gann Masters has programmed a template for this program that came with this course. The template has all the necessary table, circle and projection charts for trading successfully in the markets. The biggest mistake that new traders make, is they don't spend the time to learn how to trade the successful rules of the market. They want to get into the action of trading the market immediately.

After you have learned the rules of Gann and have proved that they work, you are ready to trade. After you have successfully traded for some time, it is necessary always to review the rules that you have learned. This constant reviewing keeps your mind alert and many times reviewing rules gives you even more insight on how to trade the markets. Every trader is different and every trader that reads the same rules of trading will trade differently. The rules of successful trading that you pick up in this course for your own trading should be written down on a piece of paper and reviewed on a constant basis. Sometimes the rules need to be changed to accommodate the current market. Keep these rules refreshed in your mind constantly.

If you are going to be successful at trading, you must plan your way to profit. You must develop a complete trading plan for the entire bull or bear campaign from beginning to end.

Copyright

Copyright 2012 by Halliker's, Inc. dba Traders World. All rights reserved.

No part of this publication may be reproduced, stored in a retrieval system or transmitted in any form or by any means, electronic, mechanical, photocopying, recording, scanning or otherwise, except as permitted under Sections 107 or 108 of the 1976 United Stated Copyright Act, without either the prior written permission of the Publisher.

This publication is written to provide accurate information in regard to the subject matter covered. It is sold with the understanding that the publisher is not engaged in rendering professional services. If professional advice or other expert assistance is required, the services of a competent professional person should be sought.

To receive a password for the Internet Support Site for the Book via E-Mail:

publisher@tradersworld.com

CAVEAT: It should be noted that all commodity trades, patterns, charts, systems, etc. discussed in this book are for illustrative purposes only and are not to be considered as specific advisory recommendations. Further note that no method of trading or investing is foolproof or without difficulty, and past performance is no guarantee of future performance. All ideas and material presented are entirely those of the author and do not reflect those of the publisher or bookseller.

www.ingramcontent.com/pod-product-compliance
Lightning Source LLC
Chambersburg PA
CBHW051635170526
45167CB00001B/198